The Birder's Journal

Mel M. Baughman

Illustrations by Nell E. Fronabarger
Text by George Reiger

STACKPOLE
BOOKS

Cover design by Tracy Patterson with Mark Olszewski
Interior design by Donna Miller

The Birder's Journal

Dedicated to Oleta Becker
who taught me to see the fossils in the rocks,
and to know the shape of an arrowhead lying
among the shards of an ancient people; who
showed me the sanctuary of the wilderness and
the perfection of all the creatures in it; for
instilling a reverence for knowledge and showing
me the need for gentleness, but especially for
giving the most precious gift of all, her time.

Mel Baughman

CONTENTS

PREFACE

Bird watching has always been an adventure for me. It is a demanding activity that requires a big investment in time, equipment, and travel. It is often physically demanding, and most rewarding of all, it is always mental. The more library and study time invested the more rewarding will be your time afield. And it is even more enjoyable when you can share your passion with those of equal passion because that wonderful formula of scholarship plus sweat plus society equals life itself. Bird watching is a lifetime of study and safari. I love 'em both.

For over eight years I carried my cherished Petersons with me on my birding safaris, and each time I sighted a new species I cribbed brief, cryptic notes in the margins vowing to one day transfer the notes to a permanent record book. Then it happened...

It was Paul Wirth's, Dick Graham's and my first trip to Alaska. Another great once-in-a-lifetime outdoor experience engineered by George Reiger, who managed to lure the three of us on at least one of these adventure packages each year for five years running. Alaska is large scale. One's "lower 48" senses simply cannot absorb the total surround or meter the swift changes in daylight to dark, the rush and magnitude of the changing tides, or the quick and violent changes in the weather which sweep across space that exists nowhere else. All of this grandeur and power also tends to reduce one's ego to its proper and smaller perspective.

It was Thanksgiving Day and the cold, emerald water of Kachimak Bay moved around the rocky point in slow, powerful surges. As the tide moved steadily into the bay, we steadily lugged our gear to higher perches all the while watching for that special bird. Bald eagles were perched in the tall spruce growing on the nearly vertical cliffs that breached from the water. The magnificent barrows goldeneye buzzed by in small formations and were often followed by flights of surf scoters navigating an unwavering course like bombers en route to their target. In the waters below we could see harbor seals rollicking like kids on their way to a candy store with their pockets full of allowance money. And occasionally a sea otter would surface and lie on his back to feed looking for all the world like Walter Cronkite munching and musing over the latest world events. That is meant to as a compliment to both, of course.

The low, heavy gray clouds pelted us with a chilling mixture of sleet and freezing rain, starting a glaze on the rocks beneath our feet and making our retreat from the rising tide a concentrated effort. We had set down our gear once again and had just nestled into the rocky nooks on the lee side when I saw them. "Ducks!" I whispered, and Paul turned to follow my gaze. (George and Dick were off with the guide pulling dungeness crabs from traps for dinner.) We watched several black points careen against the whiteness and slowly expand into shapes we had not seen before. We hardly breathed hoping their erratic course would bring them to the small cove just beyond our perch. The flat light muted colors in the distance, but as they neared we began to pick out the strokes of white on their heads. Just skimming the choppy surface of the bay, they turned toward us and streaked around the rocks and alighted on the water barely beyond the surf. "Harlequins!" "They are harlequins!" I sheared the words through clenched teeth in an effort to contain my excitement and muffle the sound. "Are they not beautiful!" "Are they not magnificent!" And I continued to describe them using that list of obscure adjectives common only to the birding fraternity like "terrific", "fantastic", and even the vernacular "wow". But you know how I felt.

At last composure came over us and I asked Paul to hand me my field guide so I could jot the date and a quick note in the margin beside the harlequin illustration. I had placed the guide on a rock between us, but it was gone. And gone with it were the eight years of notes that triggered priceless memories when I thumbed through the book during those quiet, late evening hours in my study. It probably slipped off the icy rocks and was churned into the tide by the waves. But field guides by their very nature are vulnerable to the harsh environment they are so often used in, so the loss, though painful, was not unexpected.

I resolved to purchase a diary when I returned from that Alaska trip. A book which would preserve the record of my first sightings, and which would never leave the safety of home. The book I had in mind was not available so I called upon George Reiger and Nell Fronabarger to help me create *The Birder's Journal*. With each entry your journal will become more valuable to you. And if you will spend a few moments using a set of artist's colored pencils to illustrate the sketches of the birds you sight, or even simply highlight your field ID features, such as "yellow legs", or "ruby crowns", your journal will become even more informative and pleasing to the eye as your lifelist entries increase.

We wish you much success and countless memorable moments afield.

Mel Baughman

COLORING TIPS

From the Artist Who Sketched the Birds in The Birder's Journal

My copy of *The Birder's Journal* is very important to me. I treasure it as an invaluable record of the time I've spent bird watching, and I hope you'll come to feel the same about your copy.

As you use the book, in addition to jotting down notes about the place, date, and situation for each bird you identify, I want to encourage you to sketch the markings of each bird you see. Colored pencil is probably the best medium to use for this. A small set of pencils is easy to carry and the colors do not smear. I recommend Berol Prismacolor pencils—the colors are brilliant and long-lasting.

Here are some tips I discovered in coloring my copy of *The Birder's Journal:*

- Keep pencil points sharp for control in detail.
- Note that each bird has been drawn with hatch marks to indicate a change in color.
- Color in the direction in which the bird's feathers lie, rather than in a circular motion.
- Use light pressure for softer color and slightly heavier pressure for a more solid color—but remember that too much pressure can tear the paper.
- Create more realistic blends of color and add shading details by layering one color over another.
- Use a white pencil or leave the paper exposed to create highlights.
- Choose colors carefully—once on paper, they cannot be completely removed. They *can* be lightened by lifting some of the pigment with a kneaded eraser, then using a pencil eraser.

You're ready for an exciting and enjoyable day in the field with your copy of *The Birder's Journal,* your pencils, and a sharpener. Most birders also carry a camera. Photographs are a great help if you want to add more detail to the bird drawings.

Nell Fronabarger

LOONS
(GAVIIDAE)

Loons

Evolutionarily speaking, loons comprise the most primitive family of living birds. And indeed, the quavering call of the common loon echoing across a North Woods golden pond is simultaneously one of the most meltingly beautiful sounds in nature and one of the most elemental. For other reasons, the loon has inspired flocks of "loonies" to form societies and buy recordings, neck-ties and T-shirts featuring their favorite bird. Ironically, many members of these societies wouldn't recognize either the plain winter plumage or coastal habitat of the common loon. For them, the bird is exclusively a green-headed, checker-backed summertime denizen of northern lakes whose wilderness values are determined largely by that mysterious call.

Yet the common loon has three basic calls: a yodeling laugh, a falsetto wail and, principally at night, a melancholy tremolo. This latter call is an especially haunting sound, but it haunts me in the context of the coast, not a northern lake. For three frigid days and nights, two decades ago, a band of us worked to save some of tens of thousands of oiled birds in the Chesapeake Bay. We eventually lost all but a few grebes and sea ducks. While driving one load of birds to our improvised rehabilitation station, a loon in the trunk began making its mournful cry. I drove faster and faster, but the cry got weaker and weaker, and by the time I reached the station, the bird was dead. For me, today, a loon call is an emblem of the indifference too many people show the other creatures with which we too briefly share our mutual planet.

COMMON LOON
Gavia immer

Date of Sighting

Location of Sighting

Notes

YELLOW-BILLED LOON
Gavia adamsii

Date of Sighting

Location of Sighting

Notes

PACIFIC LOON
Gavia pacifica

Date of Sighting

Location of Sighting

Notes

ARCTIC LOON
Gavia arctica

Date of Sighting

Location of Sighting

Notes

RED-THROATED LOON
Gavia stellata

Date of Sighting

Location of Sighting

Notes

GREBES
(PODICIPEDIDAE)

Grebes

Grebes are miniature loons. The two Families have so many similar breeding requirements, they become mortal enemies wherever their ranges overlap. Grebes breed generally further south than loons, thus providing more year-around opportunities for observation. Although motion pictures have made the "water-skiing" courtship displays of the western grebe world renown, my favorite of the Family is the pied-billed grebe, alias "water-witch" or "hell-diver." This species nests or winters all across the United States, southern Canada, and Mexico, and the pond next to my house seems empty without one. Every time I watch a suspicious grebe sink from sight until only its head, like a feathered periscope, projects above the surface, I am as amazed by its seeming ability to defy the laws of buoyancy and physics as I was the first time a "water-witch" put its spell on me.

CLARK'S GREBE
Aechmophorus clarkii

Date of Sighting

Location of Sighting

Notes

EARED GREBE
Podiceps nigricollis

Date of Sighting

Location of Sighting

Notes

PIED-BILLED GREBE
Podilymbus podiceps

Date of Sighting

Location of Sighting

Notes

RED-NECKED GREBE
Podiceps grisegena

Date of Sighting

Location of Sighting

Notes

HORNED GREBE
Podiceps auritus

Date of Sighting

Location of Sighting

Notes

LEAST GREBE
Tachybaptus dominicus

Date of Sighting

Location of Sighting

Notes

WESTERN GREBE
Aechmophorus occidentalis

Date of Sighting

Location of Sighting

Notes

ALBATROSSES
(DIOMEDEIDAE)

ALBATROSSES

At length did cross an Albatross,
Thorough the fog it came;
As if it had been a Christian soul,
We hailed it in God's name.

It ate the food it n'er had eat,
And round and round it flew,
The ice did split with a thunder-fit;
The helmsman steered us through!

And a good south wind sprung up behind;
The Albatross did follow,
And every day, for food or pay,
Came to the mariners' hollo!

"The Rime of the Ancient Mariner" not only embodies Samuel Taylor Coleridge's poetic genius, it contains some remarkably accurate natural history as well, especially considering the first version of the poem was written in 1798.

Because albatrosses have the greatest wingspan of any living birds, they need dependably windy latitudes to get airborne and stay there. This may be why winds constantly generated over or in conjunction with the Antarctic land mass are more appealing to most albatrosses than the less consistent winds associated with the Arctic sea. In any event, Coleridge is on the mark when he makes his albatross "the lonesome Spirit from the South Pole."

Well, perhaps, not always lonesome. My favorite memory of this family involves an outing off Washington State where dozens of black-footed albatrosses came around our boat, sat on the calm, fog-bound sea, and gobbled popcorn and breadcrusts like barnyard fowl. Truly, they ate the food they n'er had eat!

Birders are the most romantic of naturalists. We prefer the most sentimental, rather than the most factual, story to explain something. Albatrosses, for example, are collectively named for Diomedes, the King of Aetolia and later Argos, who disappeared during the Trojan War. According to Ovid, his companions were changed into birds, and Pliny writes of *aves Diomedeae*, which were most likely, not albatrosses, but shearwaters, off the coast of the Diomede Islands. Linnaeus picked up on these Latin allusions and named the wandering albatross, *Diomedea exulans*. Either unaware of or ignoring this background, American ornithologist Elliot Coues came up with his own admirable interpretation for the origin of the Family name by saying that *Dio* refers to Zeus and *medea* to counsel. Thus, the albatrosses, during weeks of endless flight, receive their "counsel from God."

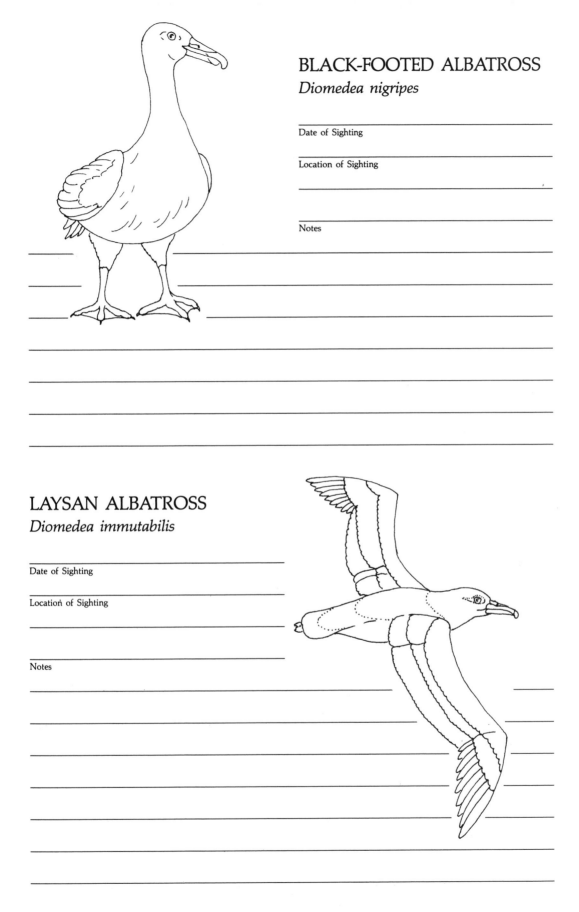

BLACK-FOOTED ALBATROSS
Diomedea nigripes

Date of Sighting

Location of Sighting

Notes

LAYSAN ALBATROSS
Diomedea immutabilis

Date of Sighting

Location of Sighting

Notes

YELLOW-NOSED ALBATROSS
Diomedea chlororhynchos

Date of Sighting

Location of Sighting

Notes

BLACK-BROWED ALBATROSS
Diomedea melanophris

Date of Sighting

Location of Sighting

Notes

SHEARWATERS AND PETRELS
(PROCELLARIIDAE)

SHEARWATERS AND PETRELS

As a bluewater angler trolling off the coast of Virginia. I frequently see Cory's and greater shearwaters and an occasional Audubon's shearwater. Henry T. Armistead, mid-Atlantic regional editor for *American Birds*, became intrigued by my reports of the latter species and asked to come along on one of my outings. That kind of request normally results in zero sightings. But

not this time. While drifting and feeding ground-up bits of bait to a school of dolphinfish found under a floating refrigerator(!), an Audubon's shearwater cruised in on alternately beating and gliding wings and gave us several passes before wafting on. Average viewing distance: 20 yards. Some days, birds cooperate very nicely, thank you.

FLESH-FOOTED SHEARWATER
Puffinus carneipes

Date of Sighting

Location of Sighting

Notes

NORTHERN FULMAR
Fulmarus glacialis

Date of Sighting

Location of Sighting

Notes

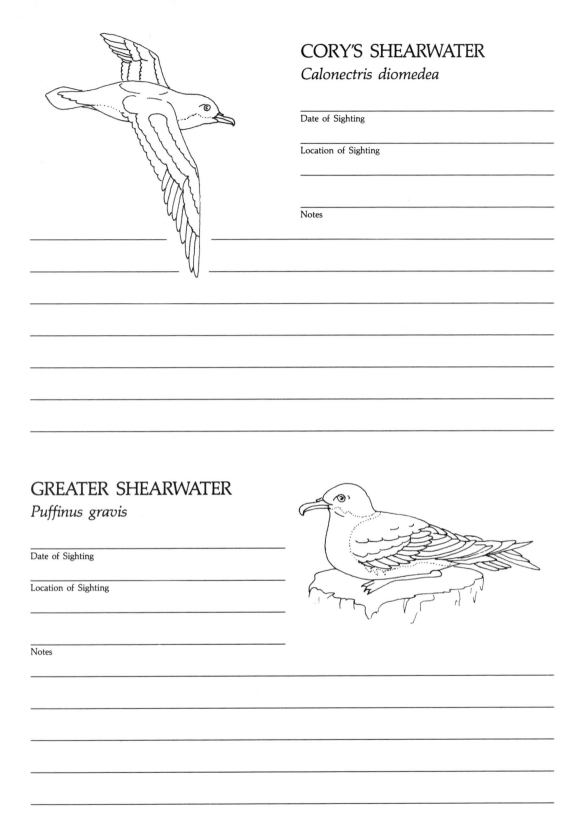

CORY'S SHEARWATER
Calonectris diomedea

Date of Sighting

Location of Sighting

Notes

GREATER SHEARWATER
Puffinus gravis

Date of Sighting

Location of Sighting

Notes

SOOTY SHEARWATER
Puffinus griseus

Date of Sighting

Location of Sighting

Notes

SHORT-TAILED SHEARWATER
Puffinus tenuirostris

Date of Sighting

Location of Sighting

Notes

PINK-FOOTED SHEARWATER
Puffinus creatopus

Date of Sighting

Location of Sighting

Notes

BULLER'S SHEARWATER
Puffinus bulleri

Date of Sighting

Location of Sighting

Notes

MANX SHEARWATER
Puffinus puffinus

Date of Sighting

Location of Sighting

Notes

AUDUBON'S SHEARWATER
Puffinus lherminieri

Date of Sighting

Location of Sighting

Notes

BLACK-VENTED SHEARWATER
Puffinus opisthomelas

Date of Sighting
_____

Location of Sighting
_____

_____

Notes
_____

_____

_____

_____

_____

_____

_____

COOK'S PETREL
Pterodroma cookii

Date of Sighting
_____

Location of Sighting
_____

_____

Notes
_____

_____

_____

_____

_____

_____

_____

MOTTLED PETREL
Pterodroma inexpectata

Date of Sighting

Location of Sighting

Notes

BLACK-CAPPED PETREL
Pterodroma hasitata

Date of Sighting

Location of Sighting

Notes

STORM-PETRELS
(HYDROBATIDAE)

STORM-PETRELS

Henry Armistead characterizes the feeding behavior of storm-petrels as "darting and fluttering like butterflies or bats—gone in a flash like apparitions—reappearing suddenly from nowhere."

American fishermen of Italian and Portuguese descent have an even more mystical sense of these birds, calling storm-petrels, "Mother Carey's chickens," because their ancestors prayed to "Mater Cara," the Virgin Mother of God. As these birds tiptoe across the surface of the sea, they reminded Christian sailors of the miracle of the Lord's walking on water.

Less imaginative, but equally superstitious, offshore anglers frequently name petrels for the particular species of fish they're seeking: "tuna birds," "marlin birds," and the like. Ironically, storm-petrels are unreliable indicators of the presence of prey large enough to interest gamefish and, hence, gamefishermen. Although storm-petrels may be found over schools of tuna and marlin, their diet of plankton makes them just as likely to turn up in the wakes of tankers and whales which churn tiny life forms to the surface with their powerful flukes. Unfortunately, in today's sorely polluted seas, powerful flukes are just as likely to churn up floating plastic particulate matter which the birds ingest and from which unknown numbers die every year!

BLACK STORM-PETREL
Oceanodroma melania

Date of Sighting

Location of Sighting

Notes

ASHY STORM-PETREL
Oceanodroma homochroa

Date of Sighting

Location of Sighting

Notes

LEACH'S STORM-PETREL
ceanodroma leucorhoa

Date of Sighting

Location of Sighting

Notes

WHITE-FACED STORM-PETREL
Pelagodroma marina

Date of Sighting

Location of Sighting

Notes

FORK-TAILED STORM-PETREL
Oceanodroma furcata

Date of Sighting

Location of Sighting

Notes

LEAST STORM-PETREL
Oceanodroma microsoma

Date of Sighting

Location of Sighting

Notes

WEDGE-RUMPED STORM-PETREL
Oceanodroma tethys

Date of Sighting

Location of Sighting

Notes

WILSON'S STORM-PETREL
Oceanites oceanicus

Date of Sighting

Location of Sighting

Notes

BAND-RUMPED STORM-PETREL
Oceanodroma castro

Date of Sighting

Location of Sighting

Notes

FRIGATEBIRDS
(FREGATIDAE)

Frigatebirds

If frigatebirds—alias, "sky pirates" and "man 'o war birds"—weren't so agile, they'd be despicable. Their grace and beauty persuades us to forgive them their ruthlessness. Even so, any tender-hearted soul who has seen frigatebirds persecute other birds trying to earn an honest living from the sea, or snatch hatchling turtles as they scurry down a beach toward the water, finds it difficult to overlook the frigatebird's rapaciousness in favor of its breath-taking aerial skills. A most remarkable proof of these skills is that frigatebirds have been observed roosting on the wing at night!

MAGNIFICENT FRIGATEBIRD
Fregata magnificens

_____
Date of Sighting

_____
Location of Sighting

_____

_____
Notes

_____

_____

_____

_____

_____

_____

_____

TROPICBIRDS
(PHAETHONTIDAE)

TROPICBIRDS

Bird-watching is much like people-watching: the more elegant the form, the more satisfying the experience. One of the most serene afternoons of my birding career was spent lying looking over the bluff on Cayman Brac and watching white-tailed tropicbirds swoop up and enter nesting cavities below me where their single eggs and chicks were hidden. In addition to being among the world's most handsome birds, tropicbirds have an astonishing whistle more characteristic of a prairie or rain forest than a seabird-nesting cliff where squawking, grunting and rattling are the norm.

A wonderful aspect of birding is that, sooner or later, it seems to single us out for that special sighting which carries with it an intimation of divinity. Imagine the astonishment and awe world-class birder Dr. Nicholas Halmi must have felt a number of years ago when he identified a red-tailed tropicbird over a Central Park lake in New York City just before a freak March snowstorm swept the bird away.

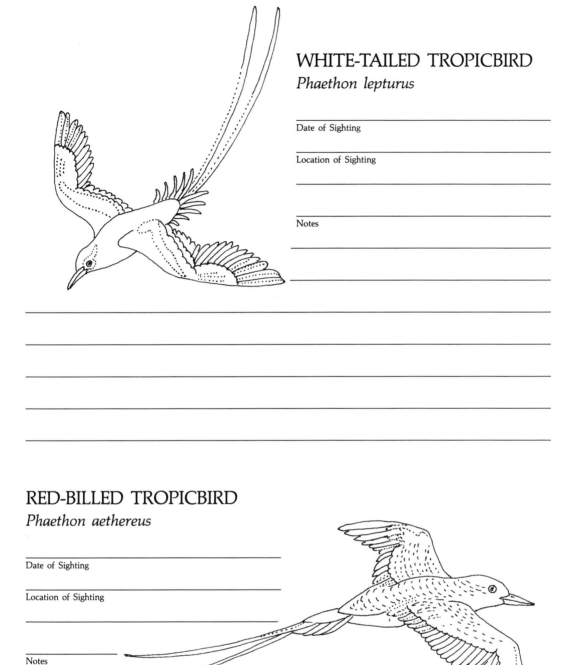

WHITE-TAILED TROPICBIRD
Phaethon lepturus

Date of Sighting

Location of Sighting

Notes

RED-BILLED TROPICBIRD
Phaethon aethereus

Date of Sighting

Location of Sighting

Notes

RED-TAILED TROPICBIRD
Phaethon rubricauda

Date of Sighting

Location of Sighting

Notes

PELICANS
(PELECANIDAE)

P ELICANS

In 1987, in a 30-million-year-old sandstone formation near Charleston, South Carolina, a fossil seabird was excavated with a wingspan of more than 18 feet. The specimen was a pseudodontorn, member of a Family that lived between 50 million and 5 million years ago. In life, it had weighed about 90 pounds, making it 70 pounds heavier and seven feet broader than even the largest modern albatross.

Pseudodontorns probably resembled albatrosses except for curiously hinged jaws that allowed the birds to form pouches to hold food for their young. Pseudodontorns were more like pelicans in also having salt glands located between the skull and eyes, whereas most other sea birds, including albatrosses, have salt glands in deep groves atop the skull. Thus pseudodontorns

are ancient relatives of the brown pelicans which still nest along South Carolina's barrier coast not far from where their 30-million-year-old ancestor was found.

The brown pelican has made a dramatic comeback since the banning of DDT and is now expanding its coastal breeding range north of any records in this century. The white pelican is, also, frequently seen outside its traditional range, but this may have more to do with expanding numbers of birders than expanding numbers of white pelicans. Unfortunately, a small, but consistent toll of both species is taken by interior hunters who mistake white pelicans for snow geese and by coastal fishermen who think it funny to rig fish-on-board death-traps to break the necks of diving birds.

BROWN PELICAN
Pelecanus occidentalis

Date of Sighting

Location of Sighting

Notes

AMERICAN WHITE PELICAN
Pelecanus erythrorhynchos

Date of Sighting

Location of Sighting

Notes

GANNETS AND BOOBIES
(SULIDAE)

Gannets and Boobies

The order Pelecaniformes includes every sea-bird design from tropicbirds to anhingas. It includes single-egg-layers like frigatebirds and boobies, and multiple-egg-layers like cormorants and pelicans. It includes birds that nest in cavities, on the ground, and in trees; birds that nest from the tropics to the sub-Arctic. The only two features that all Pelecaniformes seem to have in common are a preference for fish (in contrast with, say, squid-seeking shearwaters) and the fact that all four toes on all species' feet are fully webbed.

Yet for me, the word *pelecaniform* conjures up visions of plungediving gannets, boobies, and pelicans, of course. The most splendid displays involve gannets concentrated over shoals of herring and sand launce near the birds' breeding cliffs in eastern Canada. Although gannet numbers have steadily increased in the North Atlantic through most of this century, their expansion may taper off and even decline due to the upsurge in commercial interest and fishing efficiency for the birds' principal prey species.

When flying, gannets resemble crosses; when diving, arrows. When feeding in countless thousands, they seem to embody such eternal concepts as death, resurrection, and immortality.

BROWN BOOBY
Sula leucogaster

Date of Sighting _____

Location of Sighting _____

_____

Notes

_____

_____

_____

_____

_____

_____

_____

BLUE-FOOTED BOOBY
Sula nebouxii

Date of Sighting _____

Location of Sighting _____

_____

Notes

_____

_____

_____

_____

_____

_____

MASKED BOOBY
Sula dactylatra

Date of Sighting

Location of Sighting

Notes

RED-FOOTED BOOBY
Sula sula

Date of Sighting

Location of Sighting

Notes

NORTHERN GANNET
Sula bassanus

Date of Sighting

Location of Sighting

Notes

ANHINGAS
(ANHINGIDAE)

ANHINGAS

The "water turkey" is found throughout tropic and sub-tropic America. Although it resides from North Carolina to Arkansas and Texas, the bird is most abundant in Florida where it commonly sits with outstretched wings among the shrubbery overhanging water, or is seen swimming only its head and neck above the surface. I once found an injured anhinga in a thicket of water weeds at the edge of a savannah slough south of Vero Beach and thought at first the bird was some kind of reptile. Even close up, the creature's feathers resembled plumed scales and its head and neck, the forepart of a snake. The bird died, but so did its habitat, for the slough was eventually bulkheaded and the land around it drained and turned into a housing project.

ANHINGA
Anhinga anhinga

Date of Sighting

Location of Sighting

Notes

CORMORANTS
(PHALACROCORACIDAE)

CORMORANTS

My then seven-year-old son and I climbed the backside of a gypsum cliff in Nova Scotia and carefully peered over the edge into the nests of several pairs of great cormorants. The stench was staggering, but Christopher was enthralled by the near sight of so many seemingly tame birds and the eerie sounds they made.

No Family of birds rouses so much contempt as cormorants. Most people think of them as ugly or sinister, but without inspiring the subconscious fear and admiration that vultures do. The people who live closest to these birds are fishermen for whom cormorants are sometimes considerable competitors for the same quarry. This helps explain such unflattering names as "shag," and "shitepoke,"

One usually sees cormorants perched on pilings, ledges, and other vantage points over water where the birds can dry their wings yet be close enough to drop off for quick escape. The most unusual perch I've seen was the back of a heron decoy in my pond next to the house. This decoy impresses herons, but was clearly a flop so far as that double-crested visitor was concerned!

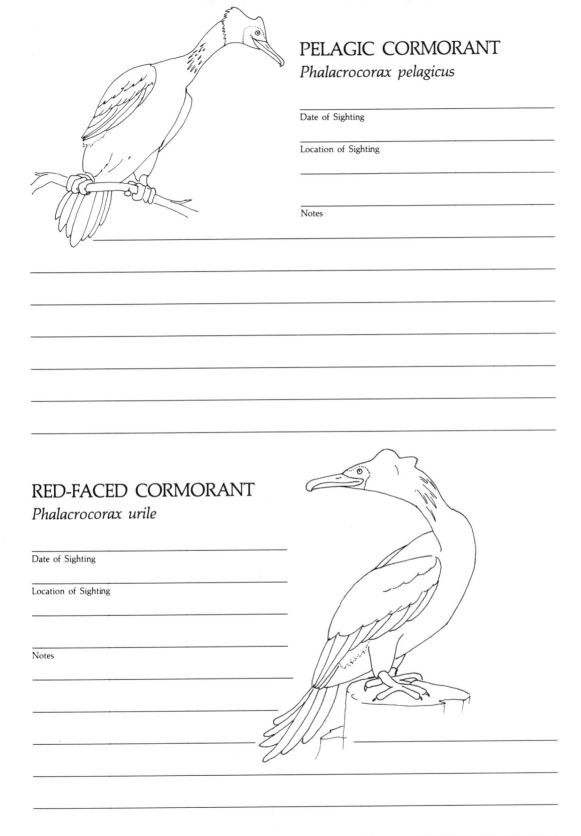

PELAGIC CORMORANT
Phalacrocorax pelagicus

Date of Sighting

Location of Sighting

Notes

RED-FACED CORMORANT
Phalacrocorax urile

Date of Sighting

Location of Sighting

Notes

DOUBLE-CRESTED CORMORANT
Phalacrocorax auritus

Date of Sighting

Location of Sighting

Notes

BRANDT'S CORMORANT
Phalacrocorax penicillatus

Date of Sighting

Location of Sighting

Notes

40

OLIVACEOUS CORMORANT
Phalacrocorax olivaceus

Date of Sighting

Location of Sighting

Notes

GREAT CORMORANT
Phalacrocorax carbo

Date of Sighting

Location of Sighting

Notes

HERONS
(ARDEIDAE)

Herons

North Americans are blessed with an abundance of herons. A visitor to Florida can reasonably hope to see over a dozen species—a fifth of the world's total. Yet just as no birds better symbolize healthy wetlands, no birds are in greater danger of decline when marshes are filled, drained, or polluted. Too many marshlands, especially those near our cities, exist in a technical sense only. The fishes and invertebrates that once gave the wetlands viability are long gone, and the muds are so contaminated as to constitute more of a threat to birds than a respite during migration.

One species of this Family which most dramatically expanded its range over the past century is the pasture-preferring Old World cattle egret. It arrived in South America in the late nineteenth century and spread throughout the continent as ranchers cleared the jungles. By the early 1950s, cattle egrets had invaded North America and within five years were nesting from Texas to Massachusetts. By 1960, they had reached California and Canada. They also spread across northern Europe, Australia and to New Zealand during the same period. Adapting to the presence of man and his cattle, this heron has been wildly more successful than its origins among Cape buffalo on the African grasslands would have forecast.

LEAST BITTERN
Ixobrychus exilis

Date of Sighting

Location of Sighting

Notes

AMERICAN BITTERN
Botaurus lentiginosus

Date of Sighting

Location of Sighting

Notes

BLACK-CROWNED NIGHT-HERON
Nycticorax nycticorax

Date of Sighting

Location of Sighting

Notes

YELLOW-CROWNED NIGHT-HERON
Nycticorax violaceus

Date of Sighting

Location of Sighting

Notes

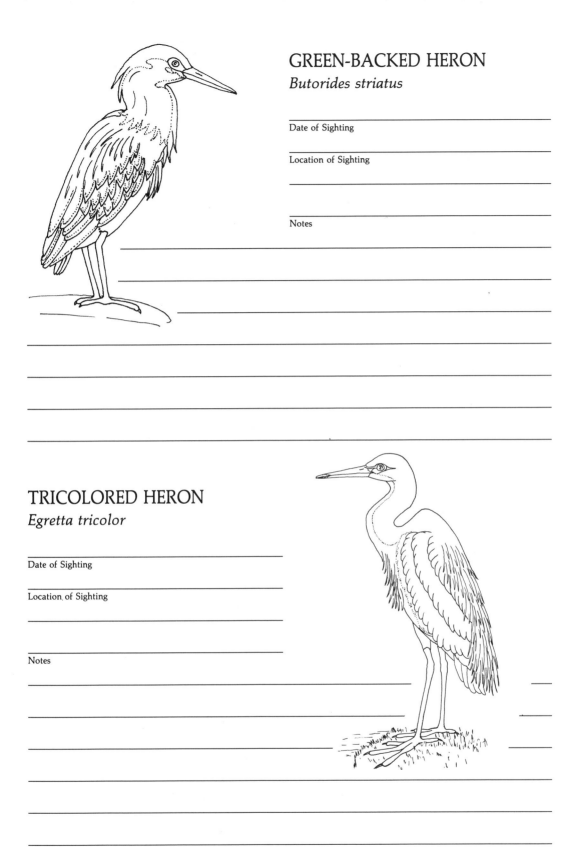

GREEN-BACKED HERON
Butorides striatus

Date of Sighting

Location of Sighting

Notes

TRICOLORED HERON
Egretta tricolor

Date of Sighting

Location of Sighting

Notes

LITTLE BLUE HERON
Egretta caerulea

Date of Sighting

Location of Sighting

Notes

REDDISH EGRET
Egretta rufescens

Date of Sighting

Location of Sighting

Notes

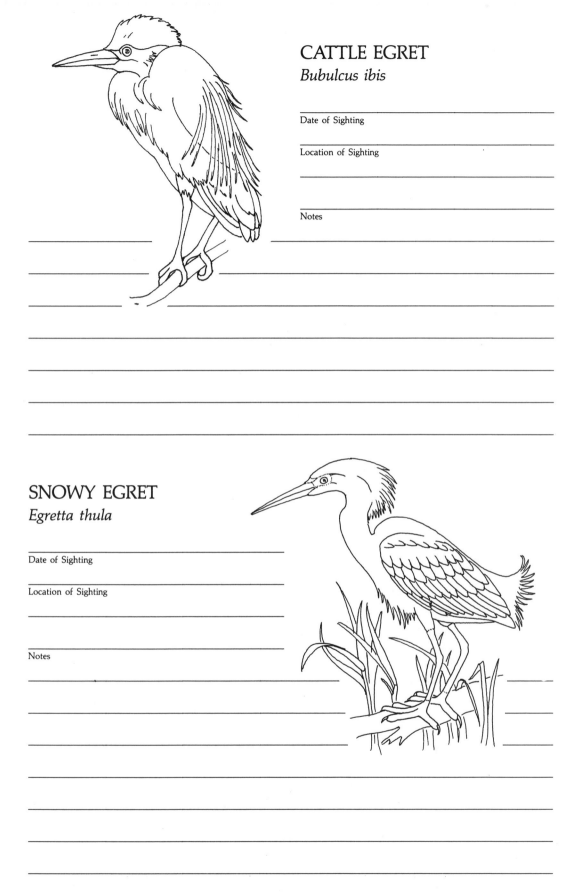

CATTLE EGRET
Bubulcus ibis

Date of Sighting

Location of Sighting

Notes

SNOWY EGRET
Egretta thula

Date of Sighting

Location of Sighting

Notes

GREAT EGRET
Casmerodius albus

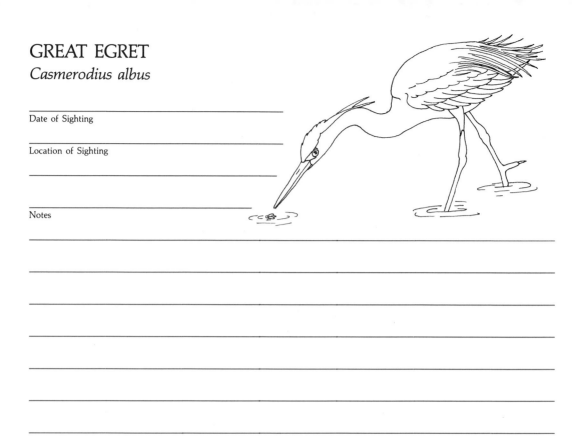

Date of Sighting

Location of Sighting

Notes

GREAT BLUE HERON
Ardea herodias

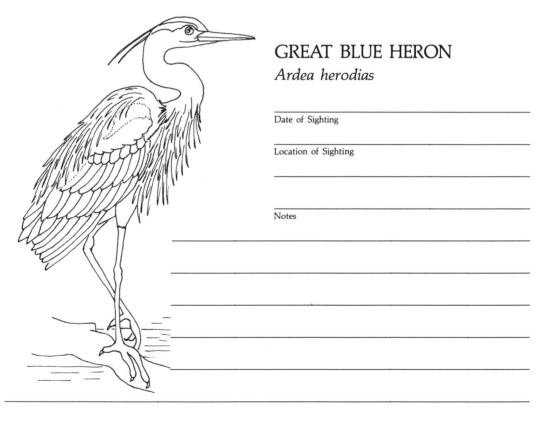

Date of Sighting

Location of Sighting

Notes

STORKS
(CICONIIDAE)
Storks

The wood stork is a fading species and one of several completely unrelated North American birds with similar plumage patterns: white bodies and necks with most of the wings white contrasting with black wing tips and, in the case of the wood stork, black tail and flight feathers as well. The snow goose, the whooping crane, the gannet, and the white pelican are the other large species with more or less the same pattern. Why? The answer may have been known to pigeon racers for centuries. They've observed that the wing tips of their white birds wear faster than those on the darker birds. The precise reason for this is still hidden in the chemistry of the feathers themselves, and it's likely to remain hidden, for despite the enormous value a solution might represent to the aviation industry, research funds are in short supply for laboratory flights of fancy featuring stork feathers.

WOOD STORK
Mycteria americana

Date of Sighting

Location of Sighting

Notes

FLAMINGOS
(PHOENICOPTERIDAE)

Flamingos

Flamingo sightings in the United States are simultaneously an embarrassment and an outrage for many birders. The sightings are an embarrassment because the flamingo's large size, elegance, and pink color make it a perennial favorite with the non-birding hoi polloi; and the sightings are an outrage because while wild strays and immatures do find their way here from more legitimate wading grounds in the Yucatan and West Indies, birders tend to presume that every stray they see is an escapee from one of the flocks at such Florida tourist attractions as the Hialeah Race Track and Busch Gardens. Yet my feeling is that once an immigrant species becomes self-sustaining in the United States—even as our own has, and even as the reproducing flocks of flamingos at Hialeah and Busch Gardens have—that species becomes fair game for birders just as other former exotics like the house sparrow and ring-necked pheasant are.

My favorite memory of a flamingo concerns none of the flock I saw while tarpon fishing in Mexico or either of the pair that flew over me while bonefishing in the Bahamas, but the flamingo I saw one January afternoon with cinematographer Dick Borden and his wife at Chincoteague National Wildlife Refuge. Dick is best remembered for the pioneering footage he shot for Disney's film on water birds. He and I had just finished a movie about ducks, and Dick wanted to get some stock footage of wintering snow geese and tundra swans in Virginia. He had just put his rifle-stock-mounted camera to his shoulder and begun tracking a flock of swans coming toward the causeway when I noticed a pink bird flying by in the background.

"Look, Dick, a flamingo!"

Borden never took his eye from the camera and completed his sequence of the swans flying past. He then put the camera down and looked along my pointing finger to where the flamingo had landed near a pod of blackducks.

"I hope it doesn't show up in the shot," he said. "Nobody would ever believe or buy a film of whistling swans with a flamingo in it!"

GREATER FLAMINGO
Phoenicopterus ruber

Date of Sighting

Location of Sighting

Notes

IBISES AND SPOONBILLS
(THRESKIORNITHIDAE)

IBISES AND SPOONBILLS

If there is a Family of birds that arouses atavistic memories of a prehistoric past, the eerie ibises and bizarre spoonbill are it. In addition to their flapping-gliding, pterodactyl-like flight, they make the most mysterious grunting and muttering sounds. There is also the diet of the ibises to consider, including such delicacies as spawning toads, newborn snakes, and earthworms drowning in flooded fields. Vultures spiraling down to a rank feast are traditional symbols of death, but a flock of ibises spiraling down toward a stagnant, but fertile pond is an image beyond death and human memory.

GLOSSY IBIS
Plegadis falcinellus

Date of Sighting

Location of Sighting

Notes

WHITE-FACED IBIS
Plegadis chihi

Date of Sighting

Location of Sighting

Notes

WHITE IBIS
Eudocimus albus

Date of Sighting

Location of Sighting

Notes

ROSEATE SPOONBILL
Ajaia ajaja

Date of Sighting

Location of Sighting

Notes

CRANES
(GRUIDAE)

CRANES

The crane's forthright appearance and its trumpeting cry make this Family the bird world's supreme emblem of freedom. Unfortunately, technology has the capacity to diminish even something as wonderful as the crane's triumphal cry. The sandhill's call is about fourth in popularity after the cry of the limpkin, the weird calls of the coot, and the laughter of Australia's kookaburra for dubbed background noises in jungle movies and films with extraterrestrial settings!

Yet, there is nothing sinister in the sight or sound of a lordly crane.

Probably the only reason neither the sandhill nor whooper were considered for national emblem status was their scarcity in the original thirteen states. I once lay hidden on a South Dakota corn field and watched a flock of sandhills circling and trilling *gar-oo-oo* so far above they seemed celestial. Although part of me hoped the birds would descend to where my hunting companions and I waited in ambush, a larger part was relieved to see the cranes fade away high over the horizon where no guns were lurking.

WHOOPING CRANE
Grus americana

Date of Sighting

Location of Sighting

Notes

SANDHILL CRANE
Grus canadensis

Date of Sighting

Location of Sighting

Notes

SWANS, GEESE, DUCKS
(ANATIDAE)

Swans, Geese, DUCKS

It's difficult for me to write briefly about this Family of birds. Indeed, I've already written two books about ducks, geese, and swans (*The Wings of Dawn* and *The Wildfowler's Quest*) and only scratched the surface of their literary possibilities. Yet the Anatidae are taken for granted or passed over lightly by many birders, as though their large size (in comparison with the more esoteric "peeps" and warblers), easy identification, and categorization as gamebirds make them pedestrian fare, somewhere between feral pigeons and herring gulls in the hierarchy of birding desirability.

But if the variety of physical forms, handsome color combinations, and astonishing behaviors is not enough to stir the cockles of a birder's heart, he or she must nonetheless acknowledge that no Family of birds in North America is of greater economic value than this one. Even in the tiny state of Delaware, waterfowling generates tens of millions of dollars in annual rents, leases and taxes. Although some birders disapprove of hunting, probably as many hunters disapprove of birding because birders pay nothing in the way of ear-marked taxes for their recreation. By contrast, the waterfowlers' obsession with "his" ducks and geese has resulted in billions of dollars in license fees, hunting stamps, and gun and ammunition taxes raised over the past half-century for a multitude of conservation projects, but most especially the national wildlife refuge system that benefits every marsh-loving migrant—including non-hunting birders.

TRUMPETER SWAN
Cygnus buccinator

Date of Sighting

Location of Sighting

Notes

TUNDRA SWAN
Cygnus columbianus

Date of Sighting

Location of Sighting

Notes

MUTE SWAN
Cygnus olor

Date of Sighting

Location of Sighting

Notes

BARNACLE GOOSE
Branta leucopsis

Date of Sighting

Location of Sighting

Notes

ROSS' GOOSE
Chen rossii

Date of Sighting

Location of Sighting

Notes

EMPEROR GOOSE
Chen canagica

Date of Sighting

Location of Sighting

Notes

GREATER WHITE-FRONTED GOOSE
Anser albifrons

Date of Sighting

Location of Sighting

Notes

SNOW GOOSE
Chen caerulescens

Date of Sighting

Location of Sighting

Notes

BRANT
Branta bernicla

Date of Sighting

Location of Sighting

Notes

CANADA GOOSE
Branta canadensis

Date of Sighting

Location of Sighting

Notes

MALLARD
Anas platyrhynchos

Date of Sighting

Location of Sighting

Notes

MOTTLED DUCK
Anas fulvigula

Date of Sighting

Location of Sighting

Notes

AMERICAN BLACK DUCK
Anas rubripes

Date of Sighting

Location of Sighting

Notes

GADWALL
Anas strepera

Date of Sighting

Location of Sighting

Notes

GREEN-WINGED TEAL
Anas crecca

Date of Sighting

Location of Sighting

Notes

AMERICAN WIGEON
Anas americana

Date of Sighting

Location of Sighting

Notes

EURASIAN WIGEON
Anas penelope

Date of Sighting

Location of Sighting

Notes

NORTHERN PINTAIL
Anas acuta

Date of Sighting

Location of Sighting

Notes

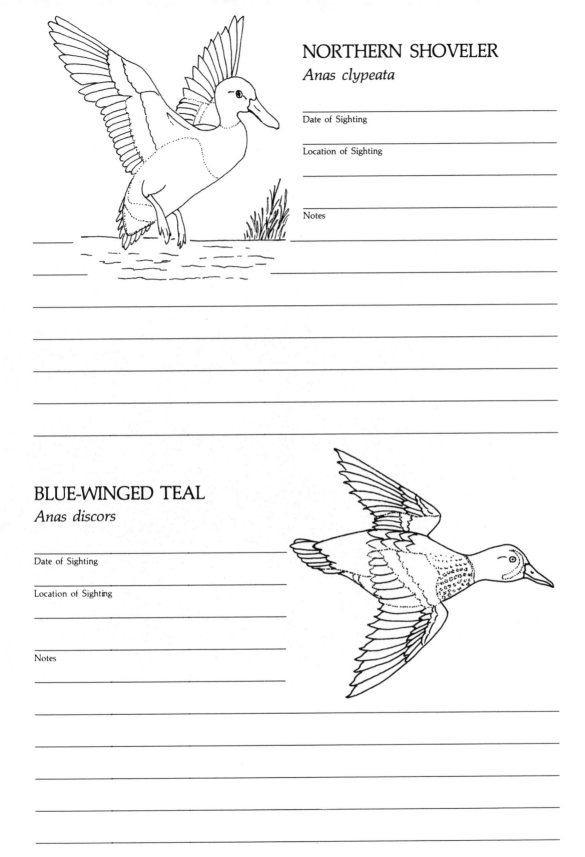

NORTHERN SHOVELER
Anas clypeata

Date of Sighting

Location of Sighting

Notes

BLUE-WINGED TEAL
Anas discors

Date of Sighting

Location of Sighting

Notes

CINNAMON TEAL
Anas cyanoptera

Date of Sighting

Location of Sighting

Notes

RUDDY DUCK
Oxyura jamaicensis

Date of Sighting

Location of Sighting

Notes

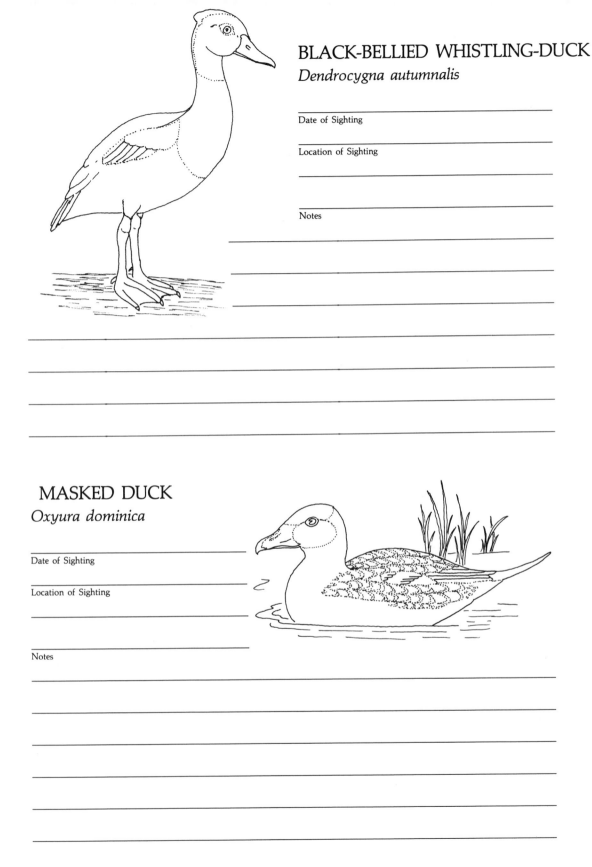

BLACK-BELLIED WHISTLING-DUCK
Dendrocygna autumnalis

Date of Sighting

Location of Sighting

Notes

MASKED DUCK
Oxyura dominica

Date of Sighting

Location of Sighting

Notes

FULVOUS WHISTLING-DUCK
Dendrocygna bicolor

Date of Sighting

Location of Sighting

Notes

WOOD DUCK
Aix sponsa

Date of Sighting

Location of Sighting

Notes

CANVASBACK
Aythya valisineria

Date of Sighting

Location of Sighting

Notes

REDHEAD
Aythya americana

Date of Sighting

Location of Sighting

Notes

RING-NECKED DUCK
Aythya collaris

Date of Sighting

Location of Sighting

Notes

GREATER SCAUP
Aythya marila

Date of Sighting

Location of Sighting

Notes

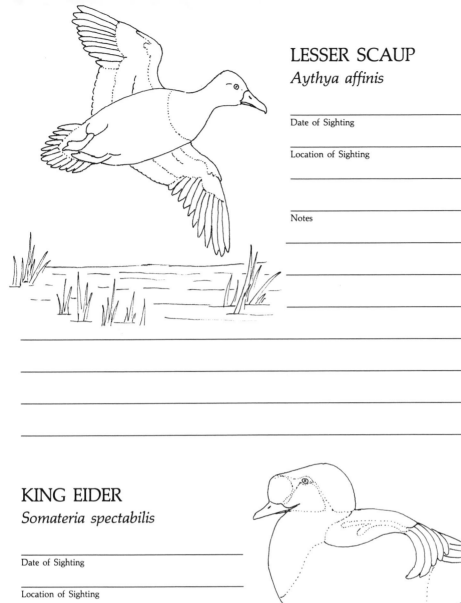

LESSER SCAUP
Aythya affinis

Date of Sighting

Location of Sighting

Notes

KING EIDER
Somateria spectabilis

Date of Sighting

Location of Sighting

Notes

SPECTACLED EIDER
Somateria fischeri

Date of Sighting

Location of Sighting

Notes

STELLER'S EIDER
Polysticta stelleri

Date of Sighting

Location of Sighting

Notes

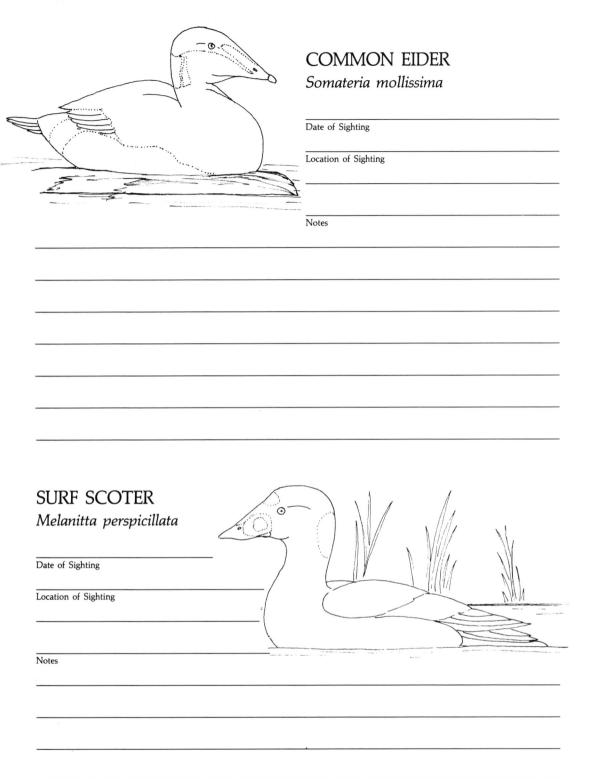

COMMON EIDER
Somateria mollissima

Date of Sighting

Location of Sighting

Notes

SURF SCOTER
Melanitta perspicillata

Date of Sighting

Location of Sighting

Notes

WHITE-WINGED SCOTER
Melanitta fusca

Date of Sighting

Location of Sighting

Notes

BLACK SCOTER
Melanitta nigra

Date of Sighting

Location of Sighting

Notes

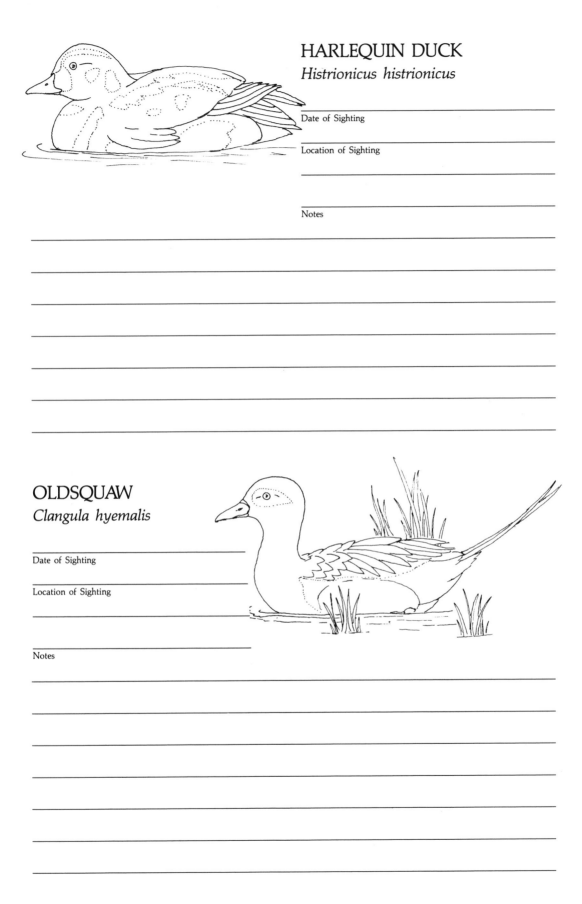

HARLEQUIN DUCK
Histrionicus histrionicus

Date of Sighting

Location of Sighting

Notes

OLDSQUAW
Clangula hyemalis

Date of Sighting

Location of Sighting

Notes

BARROW'S GOLDENEYE
Bucephala islandica

Date of Sighting

Location of Sighting

Notes

COMMON GOLDENEYE
Bucephala clangula

Date of Sighting

Location of Sighting

Notes

BUFFLEHEAD
Bucehpala albeola

Date of Sighting

Location of Sighting

Notes

COMMON MERGANSER
Mergus merganser

Date of Sighting

Location of Sighting

Notes

HOODED MERGANSER
Lophodytes cucullatus

Date of Sighting

Location of Sighting

Notes

RED-BREASTED MERGANSER
Mergus serrator

Date of Sighting

Location of Sighting

Notes

LIMPKIN
(ARAMIDAE)

Limpkin

One summer thirty years ago, I worked in Florida's Ocala National Forest, whose spring rivers were at that time one of the few places where the wailing cry of the limpkin could still be heard. Today this species has become almost common over much of that state.

On a recent canoe trip down Juniper Springs, my wife, son and I were able to paddle within a few yards of an immature limpkin. That moment was as thrilling as the sudden sight of a pair of otters swirling ahead of the canoe in the crystalline current.

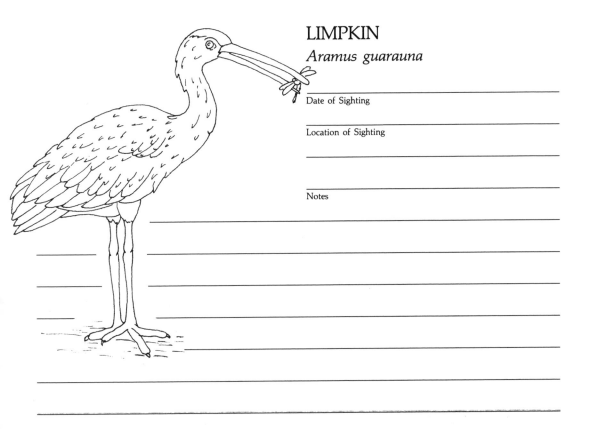

LIMPKIN
Aramus guarauna

Date of Sighting

Location of Sighting

Notes

RAILS, GALLINULES, COOTS
(RALLIDAE)

Rails, GALLINULES, COOTS

These are clowns of the avian world: seemingly awkward, seemingly silly. Yet all is only *seeming*, for their secretiveness, remarkable mobility and occasional long migrations despite an apparent reluctance to fly, and the extraordinary devotion of both parents to their young make this Family one of the most successful in the world. Their principal monographer, S. Dillion Ripley, points out that there are about as many species of rail extant as waterfowl, while the number of historical extinctions among the Rallidae (six for sure, two probable) are only slightly greater than those among the Anatidae.

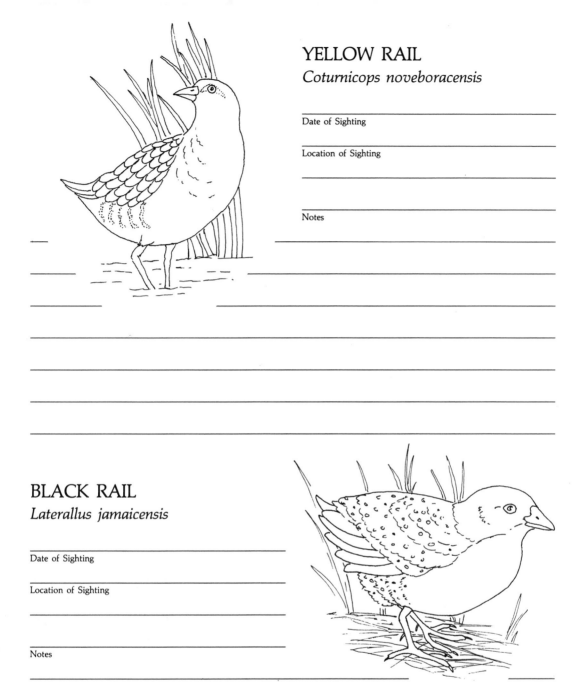

YELLOW RAIL
Coturnicops noveboracensis

Date of Sighting

Location of Sighting

Notes

BLACK RAIL
Laterallus jamaicensis

Date of Sighting

Location of Sighting

Notes

VIRGINIA RAIL
Rallus limicola

Date of Sighting

Location of Sighting

Notes

SORA
Porzana carolina

Date of Sighting

Location of Sighting

Notes

KING RAIL
Rallus elegans

Date of Sighting _____

Location of Sighting _____

_____

_____

Notes _____

_____

_____

_____

_____

CLAPPER RAIL
Rallus longirostris

Date of Sighting _____

Location of Sighting _____

_____

Notes _____

_____

_____

_____

_____

_____

PURPLE GALLINULE
Porphyrula martinica

Date of Sighting

Location of Sighting

Notes

COMMON MOORHEN
Gallinula chloropus

Date of Sighting

Location of Sighting

Notes

AMERICAN COOT
Fulica americana

Date of Sighting

Location of Sighting

Notes

OYSTER-CATCHERS
(HAEMATOPODIDAE)

Oystercatchers

Most bird species in which both sexes share the same color pattern are monogamous. The males of some, including geese, do little more than guard their brooding mates. Male rails help their hens brood the eggs, but they do not help them build the nests. Oystercatcher males, however, share all the chores from nest selection (the same scrape may be used year after year) to chick feeding. Such solicitous behavior is necessary due to the extremely high losses suffered by unfledged oystercatchers from avain predators—chiefly gulls. Once an oystercatcher starts flying, however, its odds of survival soar—which is a good and necessary thing since female oystercatchers rarely begin breeding until their fourth spring.

Oystercatchers are aptly named, for while they'll eat other forms of invertebrates, their specialized bill and feeding behavior are designed for shellfish. In some areas of their range, they pile up discarded shells, especially mussels, into middens that have fooled non-natural historians into imagining the middens were the handiwork of some forgotten tribe of man.

BLACK OYSTERCATCHER
Haematopus bachmani

Date of Sighting

Location of Sighting

Notes

AMERICAN OYSTERCATCHER
Haematopus palliatus

Date of Sighting

Location of Sighting

Notes

STILTS AND AVOCETS
(RECURVIROSTRIDAE)

STILTS AND AVOCETS

The two American representatives of this cosmopolitan Family are very different in appearance but alike in most other respects. They share the same feeding and nesting grounds and, indeed, the same principal food of brine flies during the breeding season. Yet their extraordinary leg length makes it possible for them to avoid stressful competition by feeding at different wading depths. Stilts feed in deeper water than avocets, but avocets feed more deeply below the surface by submerging their heads (and sometimes their necks) and scything their mandibles just over the bottom.

AMERICAN AVOCET
Recurvirostra americana

Date of Sighting

Location of Sighting

Notes

BLACK-NECKED STILT
Himantopus mexicanus

Date of Sighting

Location of Sighting

Notes

PLOVERS
(CHARADRIIDAE)

P LOVERS

These are memory birds. We hear their cries or see them trotting across the ground, suddenly stopping before trotting on again, and we are reminded of other places, other times. For me, black-bellied plovers stir images of freshly plowed fields in the Atlantic coastal plain, while killdeer conjure up parent birds feigning broken wings along a tributary of the Yukon, a highway median strip near St. Louis, and a golf course in South Carolina.

All birds in this Family share the same genus name, *Charadrius* which comes from the Greek *charadra*, meaning "gully" and referring to the nesting scrape. A popular name formerly applied to many members of the Family is *dotterel*. It is the word Captain John Smith used to describe the plovers he saw during his early explorations of the Chesapeake. *Dotterel* refers to the alleged stupidity of the birds attracted to lights at night when they were hunted that way with torches

and nets. Twenty-five years ago, while overnighting on the beach at Assateague Island, Virginia, several piping plovers were attracted to a campfire built by my companions and me. The birds were as fearless and persistent as moths around a flame, and I suggested we put out the fire to prevent the plovers from burning themselves. It's a unique memory in a couple of respects. Neither camping nor even access is now permitted during the birds' breeding season at the Virginia end of Assateague Island. This is because the piping plover has become a threatened species. Although the national wildlife refuge at the southern end of Assateague (known as the Chincoteague National Wildlife Refuge) produces an estimated eight percent of the entire U.S. Atlantic coastal population, the piping plovers nesting there may not be producing enough young to maintain, much less expand, the presently low eastern seaboard total of fewer than 1,000 birds.

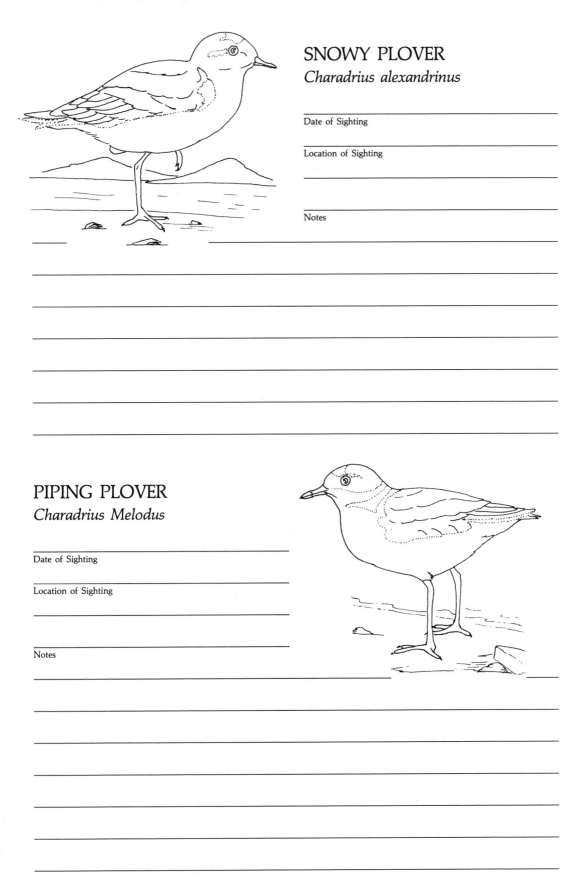

SNOWY PLOVER
Charadrius alexandrinus

Date of Sighting

Location of Sighting

Notes

PIPING PLOVER
Charadrius Melodus

Date of Sighting

Location of Sighting

Notes

WILSON'S PLOVER
Charadrius wilsonia

Date of Sighting

Location of Sighting

Notes

SEMIPALMATED PLOVER
Charadrius semipalmatus

Date of Sighting

Location of Sighting

Notes

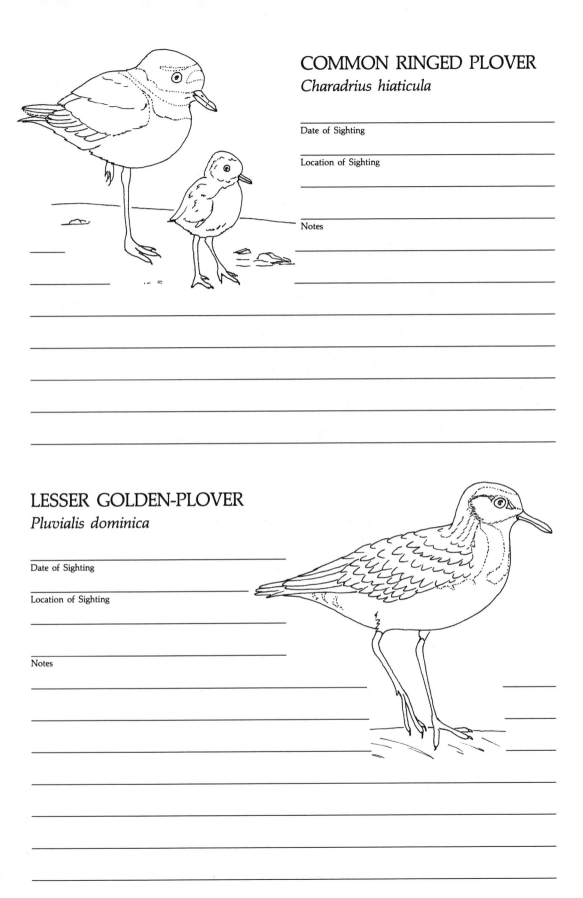

COMMON RINGED PLOVER
Charadrius hiaticula

Date of Sighting

Location of Sighting

Notes

LESSER GOLDEN-PLOVER
Pluvialis dominica

Date of Sighting

Location of Sighting

Notes

MOUNTAIN PLOVER
Charadrius montanus

Date of Sighting

Location of Sighting

Notes

BLACK-BELLIED PLOVER
Pluvialis squatarola

Date of Sighting

Location of Sighting

Notes

KILLDEER
Charadrius vociferus

Date of Sighting

Location of Sighting

Notes

SANDPIPERS
(SCOLOPACIDAE)

Sandpipers

Writer-naturalist Peter Matthiessen calls shorebirds, "wind birds"— compulsive migrants whose delicate designs and exquisite behavior refine the watery wastes where they're most often found. Despite taxonomic similarities, the species in this Family range through some of the most varied habitats imaginable—from the protected ponds and sheltered bogs used by spotted sandpipers and American woodcock to the storm-tormented seas where phalaropes winter.

Although the Arctic tern is probably cited as the world's greatest migrant— flying between its Arctic breeding grounds and its Anarctic wintering grounds twice a year—some pectoral sandpipers make longer annual journeys, flying an additional 5,000

miles from Siberian breeding grounds before reaching the Bering Straits and bending south to fly the length of North and South Americans to their wintering wetlands in Patagonia.

Birders who travel very much tend to develop a special affection for sandpipers. Our mutual flight schedules, including unexpected delays and destinations, are remarkably alike. One August, I watched a purple sandpiper picking about a cobblestone beach at the northern end of Baffin Island just 87 miles from the magnetic North Pole. A few days later, I watched a purple sandpiper trotting over the rubble breakwater at Boston's Logan Airport more than 2,000 miles to the south. They weren't the same bird, of course; but then I was no longer the same man.

MARBLED GODWIT
Limosa fedoa

Date of Sighting

Location of Sighting

Notes

BAR-TAILED GODWIT
Limosa lapponica

Date of Sighting

Location of Sighting

Notes

HUDSONIAN GODWIT
Limosa haemastica

Date of Sighting

Location of Sighting

Notes

ESKIMO CURLEW
Numenius borealis

Date of Sighting

Location of Sighting

Notes

BRISTLE-THIGHED CURLEW
Numenius tahitiensis

Date of Sighting

Location of Sighting

Notes

WHIMBREL
Numenius phaeopus

Date of Sighting

Location of Sighting

Notes

LONG-BILLED CURLEW
Numenius americanus

Date of Sighting _____

Location of Sighting _____

_____

Notes _____

_____

_____

_____

_____

_____

_____

_____

_____

WILLET
Catoptrophorus semipalmatus

Date of Sighting _____

Location of Sighting _____

_____

Notes _____

_____

_____

_____

_____

_____

_____

_____

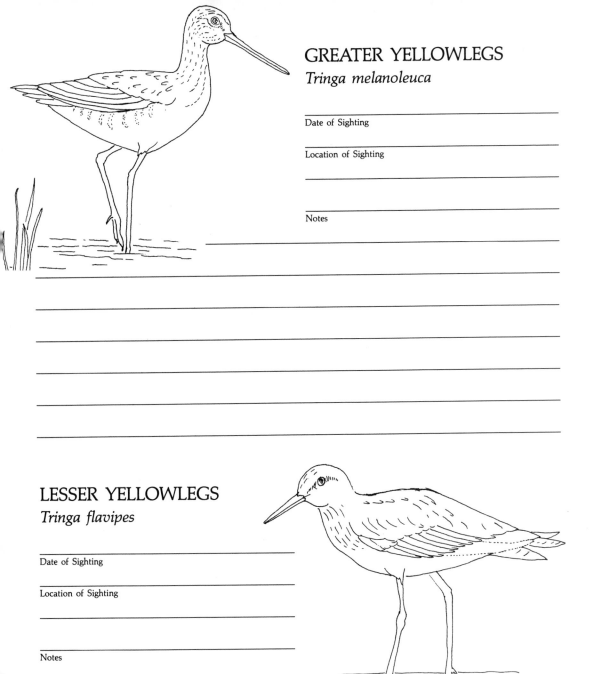

GREATER YELLOWLEGS
Tringa melanoleuca

Date of Sighting

Location of Sighting

Notes

LESSER YELLOWLEGS
Tringa flavipes

Date of Sighting

Location of Sighting

Notes

SOLITARY SANDPIPER
Tringa solitaria

Date of Sighting

Location of Sighting

Notes

SPOTTED SANDPIPER
Actitis macularia

Date of Sighting

Location of Sighting

Notes

WANDERING TATTLER
Heteroscelus incanus

Date of Sighting

Location of Sighting

Notes

WOOD SANDPIPER
Tringa glareola

Date of Sighting

Location of Sighting

Notes

RED-NECKED PHALAROPE
Phalaropus lobatus

Date of Sighting

Location of Sighting

Notes

WILSON'S PHALAROPE
Phalaropus tricolor

Date of Sighting

Location of Sighting

Notes

SHORT-BILLED DOWITCHER
Limnodromus griseus

Date of Sighting

Location of Sighting

Notes

_____

RED PHALAROPE
Phalaropus fulicaria

Date of Sighting

Location of Sighting

Notes

LONG-BILLED DOWITCHER
Limnodromus scolopaceus

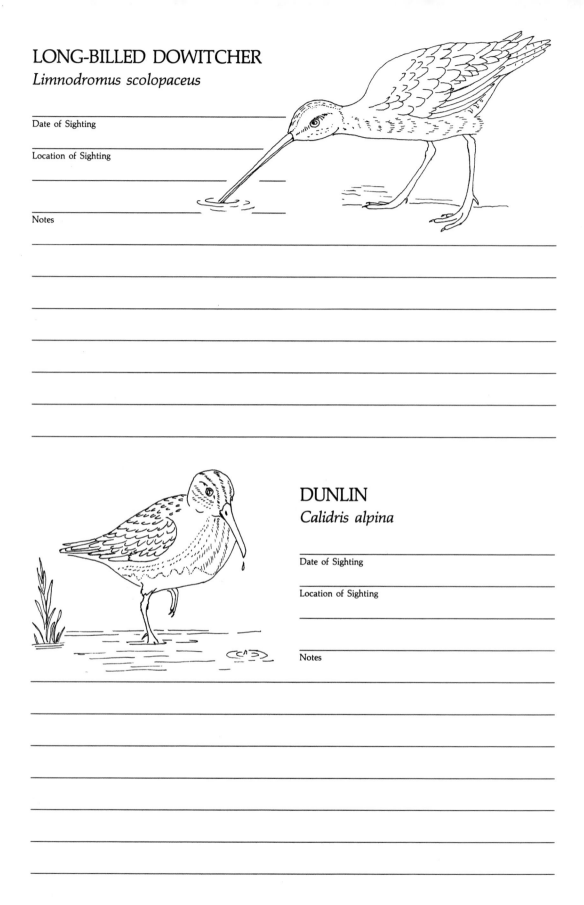

Date of Sighting

Location of Sighting

Notes

DUNLIN
Calidris alpina

Date of Sighting

Location of Sighting

Notes

SURFBIRD
Aphriza virgata

Date of Sighting

Location of Sighting

Notes

BLACK TURNSTONE
Arenaria melanocephala

Date of Sighting

Location of Sighting

Notes

RUDDY TURNSTONE
Arenaria interpres

Date of Sighting

Location of Sighting

Notes

AMERICAN WOODCOCK
Scolopax minor

Date of Sighting

Location of Sighting

Notes

COMMON SNIPE
Gallinago gallinago

Date of Sighting

Location of Sighting

Notes

RED KNOT
Calidris canutus

Date of Sighting

Location of Sighting

Notes

WESTERN SANDPIPER
Calidris mauri

Date of Sighting

Location of Sighting

Notes

LEAST SANDPIPER
Calidris minutilla

Date of Sighting

Location of Sighting

Notes

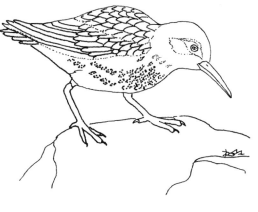

ROCK SANDPIPER
Calidris ptilocnemis

Date of Sighting

Location of Sighting

Notes

PURPLE SANDPIPER
Calidris maritima

Date of Sighting

Location of Sighting

Notes

SHARP-TAILED SANDPIPER
Calidris acuminata

Date of Sighting

Location of Sighting

Notes

PECTORAL SANDPIPER
Calidris melanotos

Date of Sighting

Location of Sighting

Notes

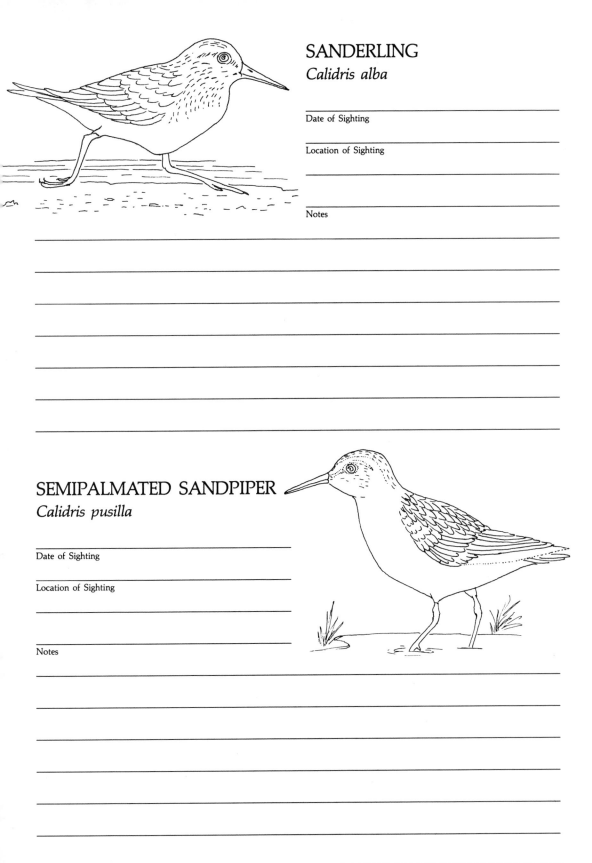

SANDERLING
Calidris alba

Date of Sighting

Location of Sighting

Notes

SEMIPALMATED SANDPIPER
Calidris pusilla

Date of Sighting

Location of Sighting

Notes

BUFF-BREASTED SANDPIPER
Tryngites subruficollis

Date of Sighting

Location of Sighting

Notes

UPLAND SANDPIPER
Bartramia longicauda

Date of Sighting

Location of Sighting

Notes

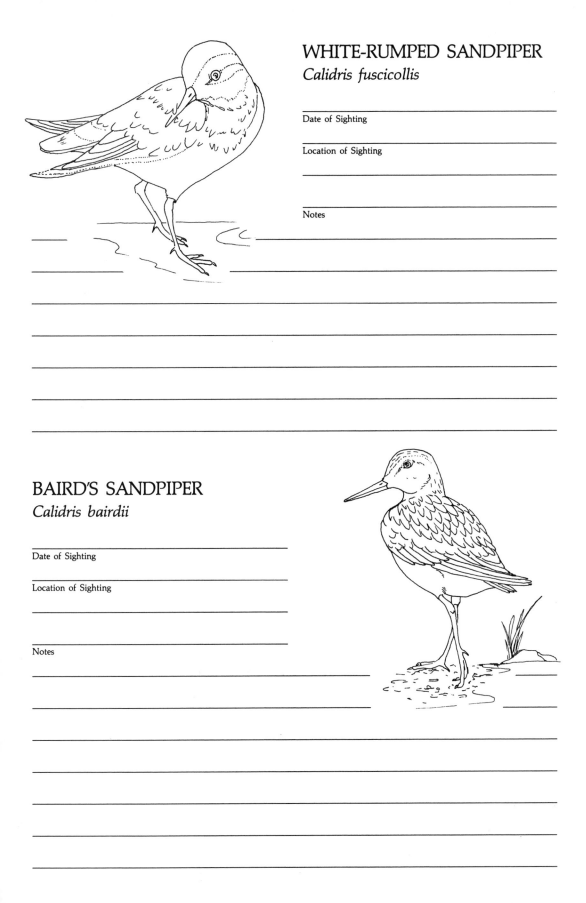

WHITE-RUMPED SANDPIPER
Calidris fuscicollis

Date of Sighting

Location of Sighting

Notes

BAIRD'S SANDPIPER
Calidris bairdii

Date of Sighting

Location of Sighting

Notes

STILT SANDPIPER
Calidris himantopus

Date of Sighting

Location of Sighting

Notes

SKUAS, JAEGERS, GULLS, TERNS
(LARIDAE)

SKUAS, JAEGERS, GULLS, TERNS

No other Family of birds boasts such a spectrum of saints and sinners. No raptors are more rapacious than skuas, jaegers, and black-backed gulls; no birds are prettier to watch than kittiwakes and terns. Along our southern coasts, watermen call locally nesting terns, "strikers," after their feeding behavior; and black skimmers, "cutwaters" and "flood gulls" for the same reason. "Sea swallow" was once commonly used to describe terns, but only sooty terns characteristically feed by swooping low over the water and plucking tiny fish and squid from just below the surface. (Some authorities even believe sooty terns remain airborne for *several years* until they reach breeding age!) Most other terns "strike" the surface when they feed. But even "sea swallow" would have been more comprehensible than the

Old Norse *taerne* from which *tern* is derived, and whose meaning has long been lost in the mists of time.

Primogeniture is everything in scientific nomenclature, but counts for little with common names. English naturalist Mark Catesby visited America in the early eighteenth century and became the first to describe the "cutwater" in print. Several decades later, Welsh naturalist, Thomas Pennant, called the same bird, "black skimmer," without ever seeing one in action. The name stuck, but Catesby had his revenge. Thanks to his pioneering observations of American wildlife, Catesby's name is known to many more people today than Pennant, who never traveled outside the British Isles.

SOUTH POLAR SKUA
Catharacta maccormicki

Date of Sighting

Location of Sighting

Notes

GREAT SKUA
Catharacta skua

Date of Sighting

Location of Sighting

Notes

POMARINE JAEGER
Stercorarius pomarinus

Date of Sighting

Location of Sighting

Notes

PARASITIC JAEGER
Stercorarius parasiticus

Date of Sighting

Location of Sighting

Notes

LONG-TAILED JAEGER
Stercorarius longicaudus

Date of Sighting

Location of Sighting

Notes

FRANKLIN'S GULL
Larus pipixcan

Date of Sighting

Location of Sighting

Notes

COMMON BLACK-HEADED GULL
Larus ridibundus

Date of Sighting

Location of Sighting

Notes

LITTLE GULL
Larus minutus

Date of Sighting

Location of Sighting

Notes

LAUGHING GULL
Larus atricilla

Date of Sighting

Location of Sighting

Notes

BONAPARTE'S GULL
Larus philadelphia

Date of Sighting

Location of Sighting

Notes

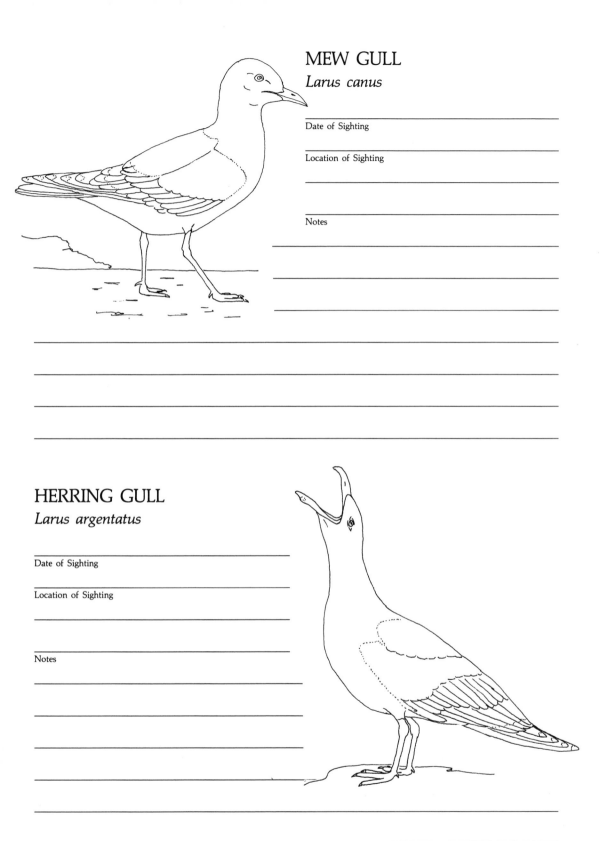

MEW GULL
Larus canus

Date of Sighting

Location of Sighting

Notes

HERRING GULL
Larus argentatus

Date of Sighting

Location of Sighting

Notes

ROSS' GULL
Rhodostethia rosea

Date of Sighting

Location of Sighting

Notes

RING-BILLED GULL
Larus delawarensis

Date of Sighting

Location of Sighting

Notes

ICELAND GULL
Larus glaucoides

Date of Sighting _____

Location of Sighting _____

_____

Notes _____

_____

_____

_____

_____

_____

_____

_____

THAYER'S GULL
Larus thayeri

Date of Sighting _____

Location of Sighting _____

_____

Notes _____

_____

_____

_____

_____

_____

_____

_____

CALIFORNIA GULL

Larus californicus

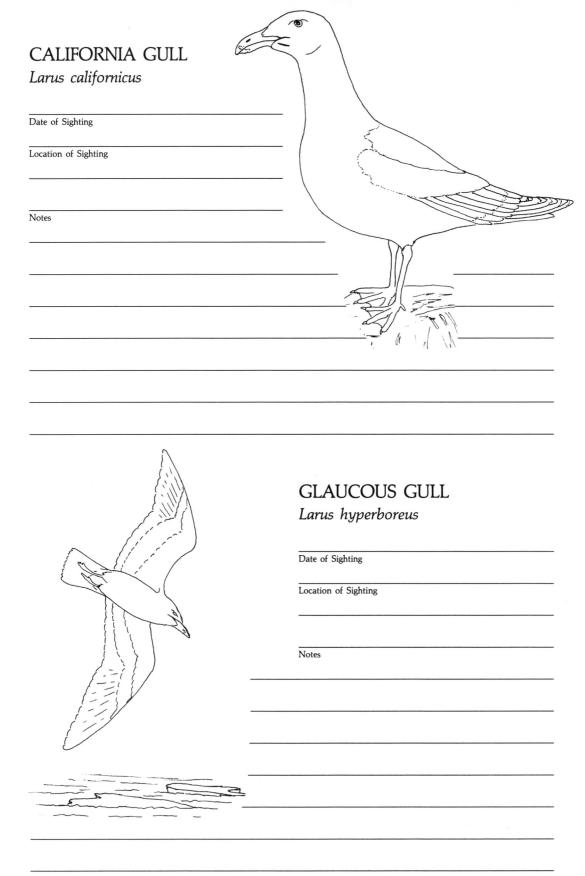

Date of Sighting

Location of Sighting

Notes

GLAUCOUS GULL

Larus hyperboreus

Date of Sighting

Location of Sighting

Notes

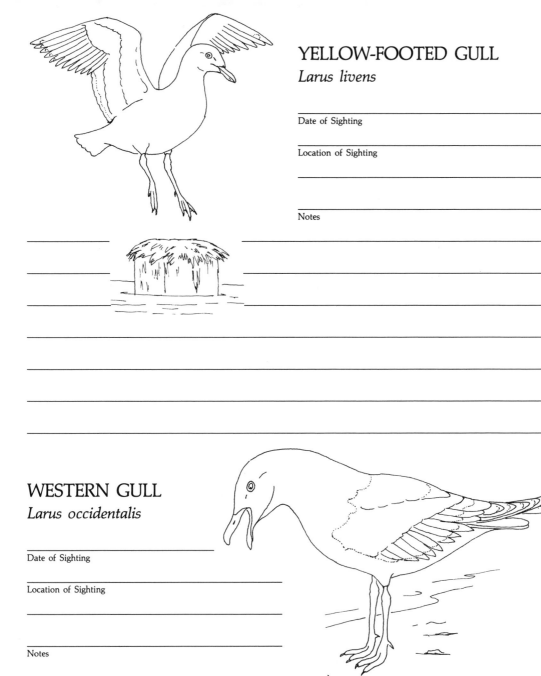

YELLOW-FOOTED GULL
Larus livens

Date of Sighting

Location of Sighting

Notes

WESTERN GULL
Larus occidentalis

Date of Sighting

Location of Sighting

Notes

LESSER BLACK-BACKED GULL
Larus fuscus

Date of Sighting

Location of Sighting

Notes

GREAT BLACK-BACKED GULL
Larus marinus

Date of Sighting

Location of Sighting

Notes

GLAUCOUS-WINGED GULL
Larus glaucescens

Date of Sighting _____

Location of Sighting _____

_____

Notes _____

_____

_____

_____

_____

_____

_____

SABINE'S GULL
Xema sabini

Date of Sighting _____

Location of Sighting _____

_____

Notes _____

_____

_____

_____

_____

_____

IVORY GULL
Pagophila eburnea

Date of Sighting

Location of Sighting

Notes

HEERMANN'S GULL
Larus heermanni

Date of Sighting

Location of Sighting

Notes

BLACK-LEGGED KITTIWAKE
Rissa tridactyla

Date of Sighting

Location of Sighting

Notes

RED-LEGGED KITTIWAKE
Rissa brevirostris

Date of Sighting

Location of Sighting

Notes

ALEUTIAN TERN
Sterna aleutica

Date of Sighting

Location of Sighting

Notes

ROSEATE TERN
Sterna dougallii

Date of Sighting

Location of Sighting

Notes

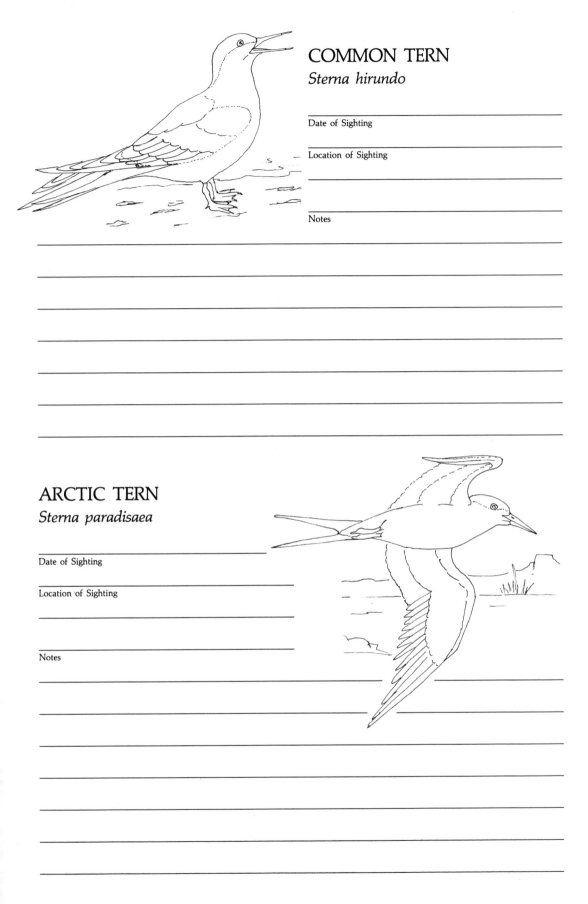

COMMON TERN
Sterna hirundo

Date of Sighting

Location of Sighting

Notes

ARCTIC TERN
Sterna paradisaea

Date of Sighting

Location of Sighting

Notes

LEAST TERN
Sterna antillarum

Date of Sighting _____

Location of Sighting _____

_____

Notes

_____

_____

_____

_____

_____

_____

_____

_____

BLACK TERN
Chlidonias niger

Date of Sighting _____

Location of Sighting _____

_____

Notes

_____

_____

_____

_____

_____

FORSTER'S TERN
Sterna forsteri

Date of Sighting

Location of Sighting

Notes

GULL-BILLED TERN
Sterna nilotica

Date of Sighting

Location of Sighting

Notes

ROYAL TERN
Sterna maxima

Date of Sighting

Location of Sighting

Notes

CASPIAN TERN
Sterna caspia

Date of Sighting

Location of Sighting

Notes

SANDWICH TERN
Sterna sandvicensis

Date of Sighting

Location of Sighting

Notes

ELEGANT TERN
Sterna elegans

Date of Sighting

Location of Sighting

Notes

SOOTY TERN
Sterna fuscata

Date of Sighting

Location of Sighting

Notes

BRIDLED TERN
Sterna anaethetus

Date of Sighting

Location of Sighting

Notes

BROWN NODDY
Anous stolidus

Date of Sighting

Location of Sighting

Notes

BLACK SKIMMER
Rynchops niger

Date of Sighting

Location of Sighting

Notes

AUKS AND PUFFINS

(ALCIDAE)

Auks and Puffins

Although all sea birds have been
exploited for food, bait, and oil by
countless generations of sailors and
fishermen, this particular Family has
suffered inordinately. The largest and
only flightless member of the Family,
the great auk, became extinct during the
middle of the nineteenth century, but
not before English-speaking sailors
exploring the Southern Hemisphere had
called an unrelated Family of birds the
same name the sailors used for the auk:
"penguin."

Although the razorbill appears to be a
smaller edition, but a flighted one, of

the great auk, "little auk" is most often
applied to the dovekie. Only two Pacific
species, the whiskered and least auklets,
are smaller. How much smaller? The
least auklet is the same length as a
house sparrow, yet it winters in
gregarious flocks far offshore in one of
the most inhospitable archipelagos on
earth: the Aleutian Islands. Its ability to
fly, its remote nesting area, and its
undistinguished appearance and tiny size
make it of no commercial interest to
man. For this reason, the least auklet is
still found locally in immense wintering
flocks that seem to carpet the sea.

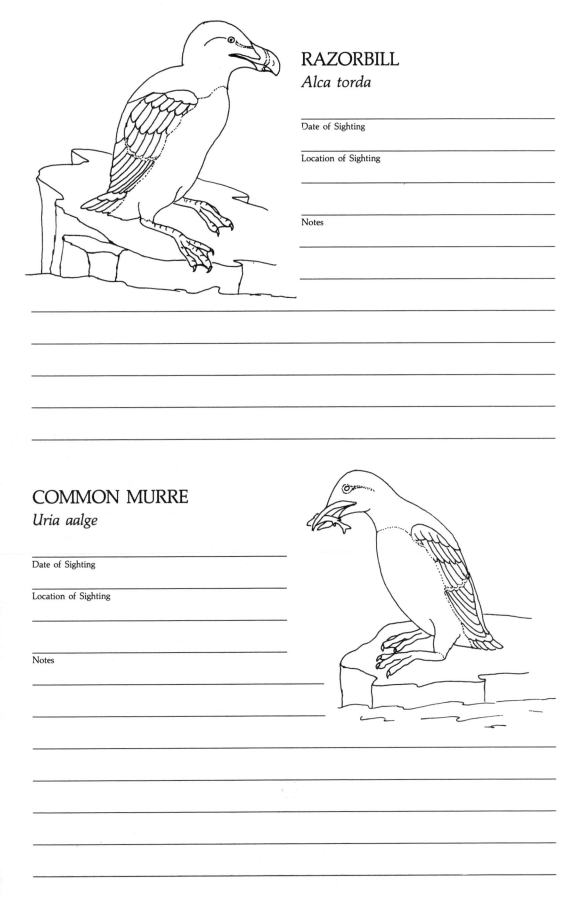

RAZORBILL
Alca torda

Date of Sighting

Location of Sighting

Notes

COMMON MURRE
Uria aalge

Date of Sighting

Location of Sighting

Notes

THICK-BILLED MURRE
Uria lomvia

Date of Sighting

Location of Sighting

Notes

DOVEKIE
Alle alle

Date of Sighting

Location of Sighting

Notes

KITTLITZ'S MURRELET
Brachyramphus brevirostris

Date of Sighting

Location of Sighting

Notes

MARBLED MURRELET
Brachyramphus marmoratus

Date of Sighting

Location of Sighting

Notes

CRAVERI'S MURRELET
Synthliboramphus craveri

Date of Sighting

Location of Sighting

Notes

XANTUS' MURRELET
Synthliboramphus hypoleucus

Date of Sighting

Location of Sighting

Notes

ANCIENT MURRELET
Synthliboramphus antiquus

Date of Sighting

Location of Sighting

Notes

PIGEON GUILLEMOT
Cepphus columba

Date of Sighting

Location of Sighting

Notes

BLACK GUILLEMOT
Cepphus grylle

Date of Sighting _____

Location of Sighting _____

_____

Notes
_____
_____
_____
_____

_____
_____
_____

CASSIN'S AUKLET
Ptychoramphus aleuticus

Date of Sighting _____

Location of Sighting _____

_____

Notes
_____
_____
_____
_____
_____
_____
_____
_____

PARAKEET AUKLET
Cyclorrhynchus psittacula

Date of Sighting

Location of Sighting

Notes

CRESTED AUKLET
Aethia cristatella

Date of Sighting

Location of Sighting

Notes

WHISKERED AUKLET
Aethia pygmaea

Date of Sighting

Location of Sighting

Notes

LEAST AUKLET
Aethia pusilla

Date of Sighting

Location of Sighting

Notes

RHINOCEROS AUKLET
Cerorhinca monocerata

Date of Sighting

Location of Sighting

Notes

ATLANTIC PUFFIN
Fratercula arctica

Date of Sighting

Location of Sighting

Notes

HORNED PUFFIN
Fratercula corniculata

Date of Sighting

Location of Sighting

Notes

TUFTED PUFFIN
Fratercula cirrhata

Date of Sighting

Location of Sighting

Notes

AMERICAN VULTURES

(CATHARTIDAE)

AMERICAN VULTURES

William Faulkner had the right idea about "buzzards," as he incorrectly called these birds. Faulkner said that if he were reincarnated, he'd want to come back as a vulture: "Nothing hates him or envies him or wants him or needs him. He is never bothered or in danger, and he can eat anything." Although Faulkner's scientific knowledge was imperfect—vultures cannot digest some forms of vegetation—the Nobel-Prize-winning novelist grasped the essence of these sometimes maligned, but always wonderfully sublime survivors.

Research in recent years has confirmed what naturalists have known for over a century: turkey vultures, at least, have a superb sense of smell. Yet so reluctant are some authorities to give credence to the idea that any bird has a sense of smell, most modern references insist the reason the black vulture is less effective at finding food than the turkey vulture is because the black species is "less efficient at *spotting* carrion"—rather than admit it may have an inferior capacity to *smell* the food.

Only three species of this global Family of scavengers exist in North American, and one of them, the California condor, no longer exists in the wild. It was our last vestige of that triumphal epoch of nature known as the Pleistocene. Just as mastodons and mammoths and giant races of elk, beaver, bison, and sloth are now found only in museum dioramas, the condor—an exquisite aerialist—is now found only in a California zoo.

The pity is that the condor could be re-established in the wild just as surely as the eastern peregrine was. It could be "hacked" into the Grand Canyon where excessive populations of wild horses and burros could be controlled on the condor's behalf. Unfortunately, this would require more courage and imagination than most state and federal bureaucracies possess. Tourist access, especially scenic flights through the canyon, would have to be curtailed, and California would have to share the condor with Arizona and Utah. Since these three states have yet to work out an equitable water-sharing plan for the region, there's little hope they could work out a sensible plan for the re-introduction and protection of free-flying condors.

BLACK VULTURE
Coragyps atratus

Date of Sighting

Location of Sighting

Notes

TURKEY VULTURE
Cathartes aura

Date of Sighting

Location of Sighting

Notes

EAGLES, HAWKS, KITES
(ACCIPITRIDAE)

Eagles, Hawks, Kites

What scientists call "behavior," laymen frequently call "personality." One of the best ways to learn about bird behavior (or personality) is to volunteer for duty at a banding station. All banding is fun, but the high drama of hawk-banding puts it in a category by itself. First of all, you must use live decoys to attract the birds: pigeons for the larger hawks and falcons; cowbirds for the accipiters and kestrels. Second, you must be alert to activate the decoys to attract the predators. Third, you must be nimble of both hand and foot to work the right lines at the right moment and still be out of the blind fast enough to catch the vigorous Cooper's hawks before they struggle free of the net.

Banding has enhanced my respect for all predaceous birds. Harriers are astonishing in their ability to dodge and weave through a seemingly impenetrable hedge of nylon mesh. Accipiters are equally awesome in their determination to attack and sometimes to attack again and again—even after they've been tangled in a net but freed themselves.

I've also learned pity for the vast majority of young hawks which don't survive their first winter. Most everything we band are birds of the year we'll never see again, because immature hawks mostly weaken and die before refining their hunting skills. Just last week I found an immature red-tailed hawk that had been run down by a vehicle while the bird was trying to scavenge a road-kill 'possum. Life's not easy for a bird of prey, and words like "courage" and "nobility" creep even into supposedly unemotional scientific literature when people talk about raptors.

BALD EAGLE
Haliaeetus leucocephalus

Date of Sighting

Location of Sighting

Notes

GOLDEN EAGLE
Aquila chrysaetos

Date of Sighting

Location of Sighting

Notes

BLACK-SHOULDERED KITE
Elanus caeruleus

Date of Sighting

Location of Sighting

Notes

SNAIL KITE
Rostrhamus sociabilis

Date of Sighting

Location of Sighting

Notes

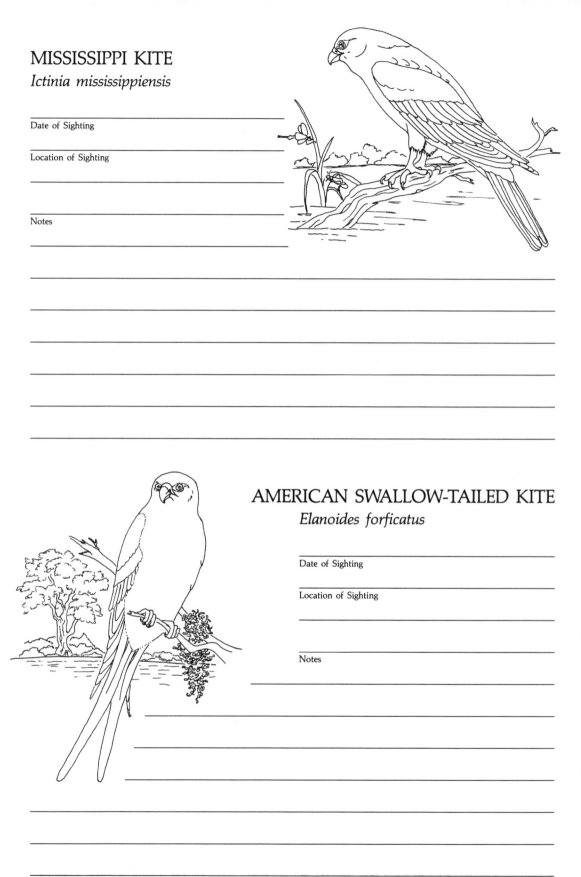

MISSISSIPPI KITE
Ictinia mississippiensis

Date of Sighting

Location of Sighting

Notes

AMERICAN SWALLOW-TAILED KITE
Elanoides forficatus

Date of Sighting

Location of Sighting

Notes

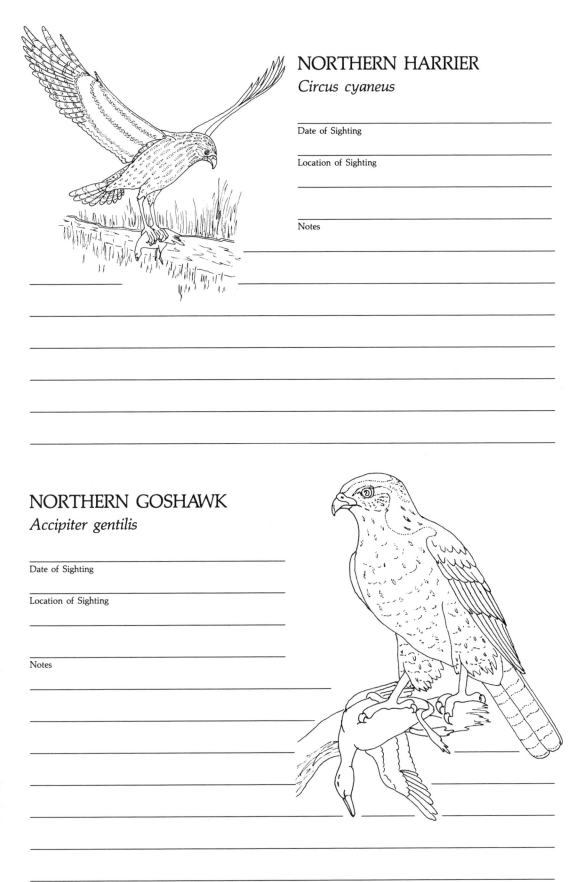

NORTHERN HARRIER
Circus cyaneus

Date of Sighting

Location of Sighting

Notes

NORTHERN GOSHAWK
Accipiter gentilis

Date of Sighting

Location of Sighting

Notes

SHARP-SHINNED HAWK
Accipiter striatus

Date of Sighting

Location of Sighting

Notes

COOPER'S HAWK
Accipiter cooperii

Date of Sighting

Location of Sighting

Notes

RED-SHOULDERED HAWK
Buteo lineatus

Date of Sighting

Location of Sighting

Notes

BROAD-WINGED HAWK
Buteo platypterus

Date of Sighting

Location of Sighting

Notes

GRAY HAWK
Buteo nitidus

Date of Sighting

Location of Sighting

Notes

RED-TAILED HAWK
Buteo jamaicensis

Date of Sighting

Location of Sighting

Notes

SWAINSON'S HAWK
Buteo swainsoni

Date of Sighting

Location of Sighting

Notes

ROUGH-LEGGED HAWK
Buteo lagopus

Date of Sighting

Location of Sighting

Notes

FERRUGINOUS HAWK
Buteo regalis

Date of Sighting

Location of Sighting

Notes

WHITE-TAILED HAWK
Buteo albicaudatus

Date of Sighting

Location of Sighting

Notes

COMMON BLACK HAWK
Buteogallus anthracinus

Date of Sighting

Location of Sighting

Notes

HARRIS' HAWK
Parabuteo unicinctus

Date of Sighting

Location of Sighting

Notes

ZONE-TAILED HAWK
Buteo albonotatus

Date of Sighting

Location of Sighting

Notes

SHORT-TAILED HAWK
Buteo brachyurus

Date of Sighting

Location of Sighting

Notes

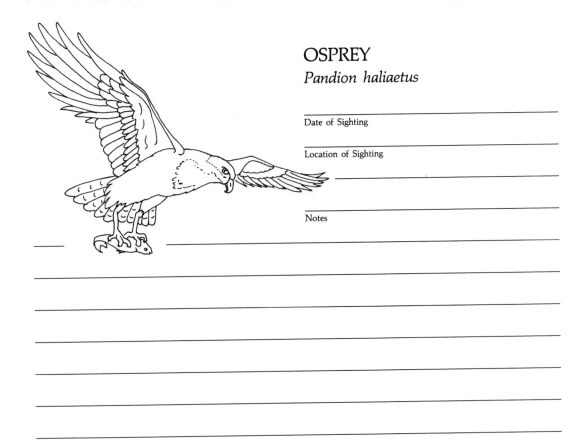

OSPREY
Pandion haliaetus

Date of Sighting

Location of Sighting

Notes

FALCONS AND CARACARA

(FALCONIDAE)

FALCONS AND CARACARA

Decades ago, when the eastern peregrine falcon was a big-fisted bird known as the "duck hawk"—before its DDT-contaminated niche was purged and partially refilled with lesser falcon genes from Europe and the Arctic—my brothers and I used to watch peregrines work the shorebird and waterfowl flocks that flourished along the southern beaches and bays of Long Island. One afternoon while returning across the marsh to a phragmites thicket bordering the parking lot at Gilgo Beach, a shower of starlings suddenly fell from the sky and huddled in the canes and on the ground around us. We looked up in time to see a peregrine strike down a straggler from the panicked flock and race on. Whether the falcon had seen us and kept flying for that reason or was merely killing the starling for its own amusement, we'll never know. But as the starlings cowered around our feet, I reflected on the fact that when confronted by its two most deadly enemies, man and falcon, the trembling starlings decided to take their chances with us.

At the other end of this fierce Family spectrum is the kestrel. A friend in the U.S. Fish and Wildlife Service and I used to enjoy banding these birds along the back roads of the Delmarva peninsula. In September and October the birds can be found perched on utility wires and feeding mostly on crickets spotted in the ditches below. Earl and I used a small, dome-shaped cage with monofilament loops over it to snare the kestrels' legs after they perched on top to try to reach a live mouse decoy inside. The device was so simple and effective, we'd often have a kestrel caught on the trap before we'd turned our car around to watch. Laboratory mice are the best lures because they continue to move and groom inside the cage even with a kestrel on top. One day, however, we couldn't acquire any mice and, in desperation, tried crickets. We put half-a-dozen into the cage and pitched it near a kestrel. Twice the bird left the wire to hover over the trap, but each time returned it to its perch. Earl and I retrieved the trap when the bird finally flew away. We found only one whole cricket and lots of spare legs and body parts. The insects had eaten one another while the curious kestrel had watched.

PEREGRINE FALCON
Falco peregrinus

Date of Sighting

Location of Sighting

Notes

GYRFALCON
Falco rusticolus

Date of Sighting

Location of Sighting

Notes

MERLIN
Falco columbarius

Date of Sighting

Location of Sighting

Notes

PRAIRIE FALCON
Falco mexicanus

Date of Sighting

Location of Sighting

Notes

CRESTED CARACARA
Polyborus plancus

Date of Sighting

Location of Sighting

Notes

AMERICAN KESTREL
Falco sparverius

Date of Sighting

Location of Sighting

Notes

GROUSE AND PTARMIGANS
(PHASIANIDAE)

Grouse and Ptarmigans

This Family includes all the traditional upland game birds. Its national economic importance is second only to the Anatidae, yet the relative economic importance of certain species within the Family has changed enormously over the past thirty years. Ring-necked pheasants were once every northern sportsman's autumn prize. South Dakota even made the ring-neck the state bird, complete with a gigantic concrete replica in Pierre. (There is a Canadian counterpart in the form of a huge sharp-tailed grouse in Ashern, Manitoba.) Bobwhite quail were the southern corollary, complete with ritualized plantation hunts bracketed by trays of mint juleps. Today, quail and pheasant hunting are relict activities,

more often done at artificially managed preserves than in natural rural settings.

The new "in bird" north and south of the Mason-Dixon Line is the wild turkey. Restored throughout its historic range and now introduced to areas where it was never before found, the turkey has become the most fashionable of feathered trophies. The top three turkey states are Alabama, Missouri and Pennsylvania with annual harvests of better than 50,000 birds each. Unfortunately, the wild turkey's success story has blinded us to the drastic decline of many species dependant on untidy hedgerows and poorly drained fields—including the bobwhite quail and ring-necked pheasant.

RUFFED GROUSE
Bonasa umbellus

Date of Sighting

Location of Sighting

Notes

SPRUCE GROUSE
Dendragapus canadensis

Date of Sighting

Location of Sighting

Notes

BLUE GROUSE
Dendragapus obscurus

Date of Sighting

Location of Sighting

Notes

WHITE-TAILED PTARMIGAN
Lagopus leucurus

Date of Sighting

Location of Sighting

Notes

ROCK PTARMIGAN
Lagopus mutus

Date of Sighting

Location of Sighting

Notes

WILLOW PTARMIGAN
Lagopus lagopus

Date of Sighting

Location of Sighting

Notes

GREATER PRAIRIE-CHICKEN
Tympanuchus cupido

Date of Sighting

Location of Sighting

Notes

LESSER PRAIRIE-CHICKEN
Tympanuchus pallidicinctus

Date of Sighting

Location of Sighting

Notes

SHARP-TAILED GROUSE
Tympanuchus phasianellus

Date of Sighting

Location of Sighting

Notes

SAGE GROUSE
Centrocercus urophasianus

Date of Sighting

Location of Sighting

Notes

GAMBEL'S QUAIL
Callipepla gambelii

Date of Sighting

Location of Sighting

Notes

CALIFORNIA QUAIL
Callipepla californica

Date of Sighting

Location of Sighting

Notes

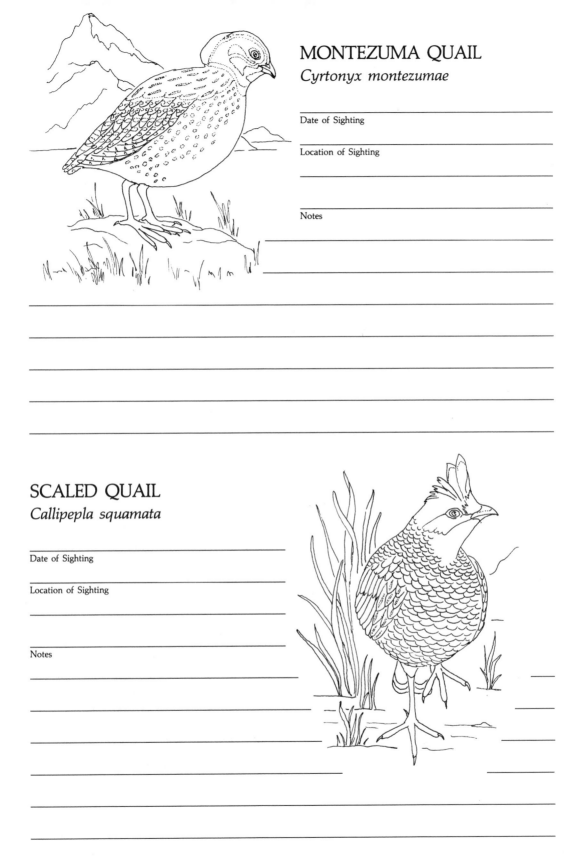

MONTEZUMA QUAIL
Cyrtonyx montezumae

Date of Sighting

Location of Sighting

Notes

SCALED QUAIL
Callipepla squamata

Date of Sighting

Location of Sighting

Notes

MOUNTAIN QUAIL
Oreortyx pictus

Date of Sighting

Location of Sighting

Notes

NORTHERN BOBWHITE
Colinus virginianus

Date of Sighting

Location of Sighting

Notes

RING-NECKED PHEASANT
Phasianus colchicus

Date of Sighting

Location of Sighting

Notes

CHUKAR
Alectoris chukar

Date of Sighting

Location of Sighting

Notes

GRAY PARTRIDGE
Perdix perdix

Date of Sighting

Location of Sighting

Notes

WILD TURKEY
Meleagris gallopavo

Date of Sighting

Location of Sighting

Notes

CHACHALACAS
(CRACIDAE)

CHACHALACAS

Modern birders and hunters have certain views of nature not unlike those held by the ancients. Superstition is part of it. The rest is a faith that in environments where so many fanciful things occur, anything is possible. Consider the unicorn. Although stories about the magical powers of the animal's horn were probably concocted by medieval traders seeking higher prices for ordinary narwhal tusk, the myth of the beast itself surely evolved in the imagination of a hunter.

Likewise, while there may actually be a creature called the chachalaca, anyone who has ever tried finding these feathered leprechauns knows they're mostly figments of a bird illustrator's imagination! I was once part of a group of otherwise sensible Americans pursuing chachalacas in Mexico. We'd been told they were a gamebird, a kind of cross between roadrunners and quail. What we'd not been told was that although they supposedly abounded in the region, no one had ever confirmed it. For several days we tore our way through the puckerbush, hearing provocative calls of *cha-cha-lac* in the thickets around us. Three of our party fired shots at birds we though were chachalacas, but one vanished after falling to the ground, and the other miraculously turned into a boat-tailed grackle by the time the collector reached it.

Upon returning—defeated—to the United States, we heard from a birding colleague that chacalacas were established through releases on Sapelo Island, Georgia. That's ridiculous! If chacalacas don't exist where they're supposed to exist, how could they take hold on an alien barrier island? So we include this species, not because we actually believe in it, but because the scientific literature swears it exists!

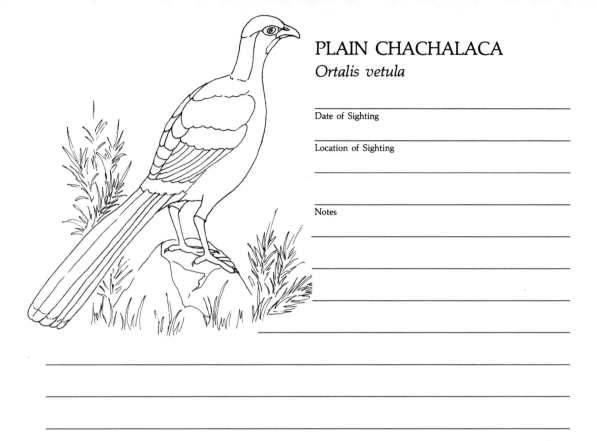

PLAIN CHACHALACA
Ortalis vetula

Date of Sighting

Location of Sighting

Notes

PIGEONS AND DOVES
(COLUMBIDAE)

PIGEONS AND DOVES

A falcon may be faster in a power-dive than a pigeon, but few birds are faster in straightaway flight than the larger members of this Family. Swifts may be swifter, but not even they seem willing to try to outfly a pursuing falcon as pigeons nearly always do. Since a majority of such straightaway chases end with the pigeon victorious, falcons seem to take a special delight in power-diving pigeons whenever they can get above them.

Although mourning and spotted doves are the most streamlined members of the Family, they are not necessarily the fastest, for the simple physical reason that among birds of the same general design, the ones with the largest wing surfaces and deepest breasts are the most swift. Indeed, the Smithsonian Institution has a mounted racing pigeon (a refined version of the rock dove) that was clocked at over 90 miles per hour in straightaway flight on a calm day. A mourning dove needs a tail wind to reach even 70 mph.

ROCK DOVE
Columba livia

Date of Sighting

Location of Sighting

Notes

BAND-TAILED PIGEON
Columba fasciata

Date of Sighting

Location of Sighting

Notes

WHITE-CROWNED PIGEON
Columba leucocephala

Date of Sighting

Location of Sighting

Notes

SPOTTED DOVE
Streptopelia chinensis

Date of Sighting

Location of Sighting

Notes

INCA DOVE
Columbina inca

Date of Sighting

Location of Sighting

Notes

MOURNING DOVE
Zenaida macroura

Date of Sighting

Location of Sighting

Notes

WHITE-WINGED DOVE
Zenaida asiatica

Date of Sighting

Location of Sighting

Notes

COMMON GROUND-DOVE
Columbina passerina

Date of Sighting

Location of Sighting

Notes

WHITE-TIPPED DOVE
Leptotila verreauxi

Date of Sighting

Location of Sighting

Notes

CUCKOOS AND ANIS
(CUCULIDAE)

Cuckoos and Anis

Laymen are puzzled as to why such very different physical types as anis, cuckoos and roadrunners are lumped into one Family. The mumbo-jumbo about toe configuration—two pointing forward, two back—is too subtle for the average person who sees that anis resemble grackles far more than they do roadrunners.

Yet anis are this Family's link with parrots; which are in turn the evolutionary link between pigeons and cuckoos. Anis and parrots share thickened bills and gregarious behavior. At the same time, an aspect of the anis' gregariousness, points to the cuckoo: female anis frequently use group nests with as many as two dozen eggs in a single nest.

Cuculidae are a puzzlement for other reasons. Cuckoos, for example, may resemble one another more than they do anis and roadrunners, but not even the cuckoos have similar behavioral traits. The common cuckoo is world reknown, not only for its *cuc-koo* clock call, but for parasitizing a broad spectrum of other birds' nests with its eggs. This species has even evolved varieties which parasitize Europe's reed warbler, meadow pipit, and pied wagtail nests with eggs matching the different color patterns of their victims' eggs. By contrast, North American yellow-billed and black-billed cuckoos build nests and raise their young the old-fashioned way. Best of all, they even feast on the agriculturally destructive "hairy" caterpillars that most other birds avoid.

BLACK-BILLED CUCKOO
Coccyzus erythropthalmus

Date of Sighting

Location of Sighting

Notes

GREATER ROADRUNNER
Geococcyx californianus

Date of Sighting

Location of Sighting

Notes

MANGROVE CUCKOO
Coccyzus minor

Date of Sighting

Location of Sighting

Notes

YELLOW-BILLED CUCKOO
Coccyzus americanus

Date of Sighting

Location of Sighting

Notes

GROOVE-BILLED ANI
Crotophaga sulcirostris

Date of Sighting

Location of Sighting

Notes

SMOOTH-BILLED ANI
Crotophaga ani

Date of Sighting

Location of Sighting

Notes

OWLS
(TYTONIDAE AND STRIGIDAE)

Owls

Some birds are more often heard than seen. This is especially true of the nocturnal owls and nightjars. But whereas the breeding calls of nightjars appeal sweetly to the ears of most human listeners, no owl call—not even the trill of a screech owl—seems to do less than send shivers up the spine.

Certainly the call of the great horned owl must cause its prey to shiver. Some authorities even suggest that owls intentionally try to frighten their prey into moving by calling. Since calls made too close to dawn, however, do little more than invite the retribution of mobbing prey species such as crows for horned owls and songbirds for screech owls, I'm skeptical that any owl would voluntarily give away its position to any creature but another owl, and then only during the breeding season.

When I was a youngster, great horned owls were protected in none of our states or provinces, and some counties still offered bounties on this poultry-killing predator. Today, all raptors are protected throughout North America, and some people blame the increasing numbers of great horned owls for the decline of some gamebirds and rabbits. As is always the case, however, habitat destruction and degradation are the principal culprits in any species' decline. Furthermore, the bipartisan taste of great horned owls means that while they may make local inroads on patrician pheasants and wild ducks, the owls also opportunistically kill plebian skunks and feral cats.

LONG-EARED OWL
Asio otus

Date of Sighting

Location of Sighting

Notes

GREAT HORNED OWL
Bubo virginianus

Date of Sighting

Location of Sighting

Notes

COMMON BARN OWL
Tyto alba

Date of Sighting

Location of Sighting

Notes

SHORT-EARED OWL
Asio flammeus

Date of Sighting

Location of Sighting

Notes

SPOTTED OWL
Strix occidentalis

Date of Sighting

Location of Sighting

Notes

SNOWY OWL
Nyctea scandiaca

Date of Sighting

Location of Sighting

Notes

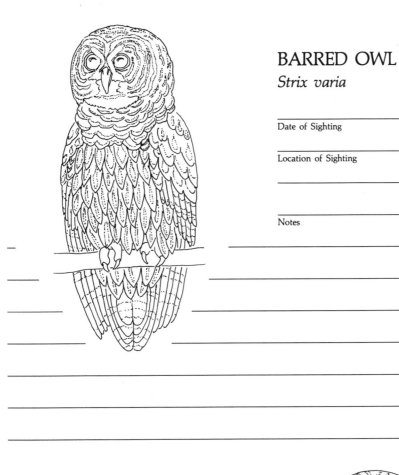

BARRED OWL
Strix varia

Date of Sighting

Location of Sighting

Notes

GREAT GRAY OWL
Strix nebulosa

Date of Sighting

Location of Sighting

Notes

WHISKERED SCREECH-OWL
Otus trichopsis

Date of Sighting

Location of Sighting

Notes

FLAMMULATED OWL
Otus flammeolus

Date of Sighting

Location of Sighting

Notes

EASTERN SCREECH-OWL
Otus asio

Date of Sighting

Location of Sighting

Notes

WESTERN SCREECH-OWL
Otus kennicotti

Date of Sighting

Location of Sighting

Notes

NORTHERN PYGMY-OWL
Glaucidium gnoma

Date of Sighting

Location of Sighting

Notes

NORTHERN SAW-WHET OWL
Aegolius acadicus

Date of Sighting

Location of Sighting

Notes

ELF OWL
Micrathene whitneyi

Date of Sighting

Location of Sighting

Notes

FERRUGINOUS PYGMY-OWL
Glaucidium brasilianum

Date of Sighting

Location of Sighting

Notes

BURROWING OWL
Athene cunicularia

Date of Sighting

Location of Sighting

Notes

NORTHERN HAWK-OWL
Surnia ulula

Date of Sighting

Location of Sighting

Notes

BOREAL OWL
Aegolius funereus

Date of Sighting

Location of Sighting

Notes

NIGHTJARS
(CAPRIMULGIDAE)

NIGHTJARS

One enchanted evening under a full moon sky, my family and I stalked several chuck-will's-widows close enough to hear clearly the sibilant *chuck* in their calls, yet not so close to flush the birds. So quietly do nightjars take wing, you're never sure whether the birds are still there unless you hear them call again. And so ventriloquistic is the nightjar's ability to "throw" its call, a bird may sound a hundred yards away one moment and underfoot the next.

Once while collecting moths by shining a light against a sheet hung between two trees, a chuck-will's-widow swooped in and caught several of my largest potential specimens. I was reminded of reports that this largest of all the nightjars has caught and swallowed songbirds. If that happens, it's an uncommon occurrence, not so much because a 12-inch chuck-will's-widow would have trouble swallowing a 4-inch kinglet, than because the nocturnal flight of the former doesn't often cross the diurnal path of the latter.

My favorite memory of nightjars has more to do with angling than birding. One June evening I caught a 17-inch rainbow trout on a dry fly so tiny I couldn't see it floating on the surface of Montana's Flathead River. When I hooked the trout, "bull bats," a name derived from the sound male nighthawks make while diving toward the earth in their courtship flights, became my cheering section beyond the willows bordering the river. My reel sang, the trout leaped and splashed, and "the bullbats bellowed." The magic of the moment was enhanced by my knowledge that the booming chorus had only recently come from Argentina and Brazil.

CHUCK-WILL'S-WIDOW
Caprimulgus carolinensis

Date of Sighting

Location of Sighting

Notes

WHIP-POOR-WILL
Caprimulgus vociferus

Date of Sighting

Location of Sighting

Notes

COMMON POORWILL
Phalaenoptilus nuttallii

Date of Sighting

Location of Sighting

Notes

COMMON NIGHTHAWK
Chordeiles minor

Date of Sighting

Location of Sighting

Notes

LESSER NIGHTHAWK
Chordeiles acutipennis

Date of Sighting

Location of Sighting

Notes

SWIFTS
(APODIDAE)

Swifts

One wonders what chimney swifts did before there were chimneys. This expanding habitat undoubtedly saved them from a catastrophic decline during the nineteenth century when the great eastern forests (and hollow nesting trees) were being cleared. Chimneys may even be better habitat than trees. Swifts return from Peru about the time the last woodstove fires of the North American winter have been burned. They leave again well before the first fires are lit. In the meantime, they have a soot-sanitized and predator-free environment in which to raise their young.

Blacksnakes are the bane of every tree- and abandoned-house nesting bird. No homeowner condones blacksnakes crawling through his kneewalls and up his chimneys. So long as the homeowner knows that the buzzing noises reverberating from his hearth are made by chimney swifts and not snakes, raccoons, or other predators, the swifts are safer than they'd be in a hollow tree.

CHIMNEY SWIFT
Chaetura pelagica

Date of Sighting

Location of Sighting

Notes

BLACK SWIFT
Cypseloides niger

Date of Sighting

Location of Sighting

Notes

VAUX'S SWIFT
Chaetura vauxi

Date of Sighting

Location of Sighting

Notes

WHITE-THROATED SWIFT
Aeronautes saxatalis

Date of Sighting

Location of Sighting

Notes

HUMMINGBIRDS
(TROCHILIDAE)

Hummingbirds

When we examine evolutionary shrubs, we see that branches are generally thinner (meaning fewer species) and more specialized the further they grow from the main stem. There are fewer chachalacas in the world, for example—which closely resemble one another—than there are grouse, ptarmigan and quail.

Yet birds offer exceptions to every rule, and no Family is more emblematic of exceptions than the hummingbirds. So recently evolved as to comprise genera found exclusively in the New World, there are nearly 600 species and subspecies of these highly specialized feeders and breeders found from the deepest rain forests of the tropics to the highest mountain meadows of our temperate zones. The rufous hummingbird has even adapted itself to annual migrations between Latin American jungles and Alaskan forests.

The most familiar of the clan and the only one found regularly east of the Mississippi is the ruby-throat. The homeowner's love of this species has spawned a veritable cult of the hummingbird, complete with elaborate hanging feeders and secret sugar-water formulae. My wife and I were novices of the cult for a number of summers, but we always seemed to get our feeders up too early or too late. Or at least we thought they were too late.

In the spring, when the birds first arrive, many appropriate food sources such as weigela are in bloom, and hanging feeders are less crucial than later in the summer—especially a hot summer—when the moisture of the sugar-water is nearly as valuable as the high-energy sugar itself. At the peak of one miserable August heat wave, my wife and I found a dead and sadly dehydrated male hummingbird in our garage. My wife set out feeders again, and we were quickly rewarded with thirsty, grateful ruby-throats.

LUCIFER HUMMINGBIRD
Calothorax lucifer

Date of Sighting

Location of Sighting

Notes

BROAD-BILLED HUMMINGBIRD
Cynanthus latirostris

Date of Sighting

Location of Sighting

Notes

BUFF-BELLIED HUMMINGBIRD
Amazilia yucatanensis

Date of Sighting

Location of Sighting

Notes

BERYLLINE HUMMINGBIRD
Amazilia beryllina

Date of Sighting

Location of Sighting

Notes

BLUE-THROATED HUMMINGBIRD
Lampornis clemenciae

Date of Sighting

Location of Sighting

Notes

MAGNIFICENT HUMMINGBIRD
Eugenes fulgens

Date of Sighting

Location of Sighting

Notes

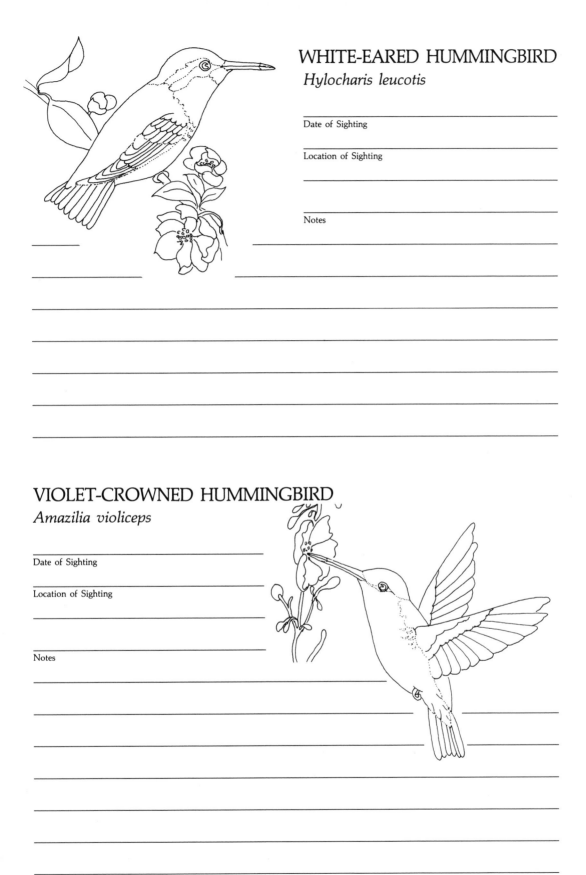

WHITE-EARED HUMMINGBIRD
Hylocharis leucotis

Date of Sighting

Location of Sighting

Notes

VIOLET-CROWNED HUMMINGBIRD
Amazilia violiceps

Date of Sighting

Location of Sighting

Notes

COSTA'S HUMMINGBIRD
Calypte costae

Date of Sighting

Location of Sighting

Notes

ANNA'S HUMMINGBIRD
Calypte anna

Date of Sighting

Location of Sighting

Notes

RUBY-THROATED HUMMINGBIRD
Archilochus colubris

Date of Sighting

Location of Sighting

Notes

BLACK-CHINNED HUMMINGBIRD
Archilochus alexandri

Date of Sighting

Location of Sighting

Notes

RUFOUS HUMMINGBIRD
Selaphorus rufus

Date of Sighting

Location of Sighting

Notes

ALLEN'S HUMMINGBIRD
Selasphorus sasin

Date of Sighting

Location of Sighting

Notes

CALLIOPE HUMMINGBIRD
Stellula calliope

Date of Sighting

Location of Sighting

Notes

BROAD-TAILED HUMMINGBIRD
Selasphorus platycercus

Date of Sighting

Location of Sighting

Notes

KINGFISHERS
(ALCEDINIDAE)

KINGFISHERS

Wherever I've traveled in the world—Argentina or Australia, South Africa or South Vietnam—I've been greeted by the boastful cry and flamboyant behavior of a kingfisher. Every member of this cosmopolitan Family is a cheerful sight, but none more cheering than our coast-to-coast resident, the belted kingfisher.

The spring after I dug a pond next to my house, a pair of kingfishers dug their nesting burrow in the dike separating the freshwater impoundment from the salt marsh beyond. They successfully brought off a brood that first year and intermittently for several years thereafter. But the sandy core of the dike must have proved too unstable, or predators too persistent, for kingfishers have not nested here for a number of years. Still, the birds regularly fish the pond with one or two great blue herons. The unrelated species share the same habitat year around—although the kingfisher has less capacity to survive extreme winters than its larger and less active associate, the heron.

BELTED KINGFISHER
Ceryle alcyon

Date of Sighting

Location of Sighting

Notes

RINGED KINGFISHER
Ceryle torquata

Date of Sighting

Location of Sighting

Notes

GREEN KINGFISHER
Chloroceryle americana

Date of Sighting

Location of Sighting

Notes

WOODPECKERS
(PICIDAE)

Woodpeckers

There are few reasons a person has for spending hours sitting still in the middle of a woods. Most people outdoors are so active, they don't have time to watch birds, only to see them.

Deer hunting provides ample opportunity to watch as well as to see. While sitting a dozen or more feet up a tree, I observe a surprising variety of birds. Among the most common are woodpeckers. The publisher of this book once reported seeing five different species in less than an hour from a Virginia stand: hairy, downy, red-bellied, yellow-bellied sapsucker, and pileated. The only two he might have seen, but didn't, were the northern flicker and red-headed woodpecker. Although Mel didn't see a buck that afternoon, the outing was his most memorable of the season.

Sometimes we get so involved watching birds, we forget what we're supposed to be doing. Or, perhaps, deer hunting is only an excuse we sometimes give for watching birds. Once while sitting in new-fallen snow on the side of a Pennsylvania mountain, I was joined by a pileated woodpecker in a tree just down the steep slope so the bird was near my eye level. The woodpecker immediately began excavating rotted wood. Its vigorous activity was so fascinatingly noisy, I never saw the deer

that walked by less than ten steps away and whose tracks I discovered only after I got up to go back to the cabin at mid-morning—long after both the woodpecker and deer had departed.

The pileated woodpecker is what ecologists call an "indicator species." Each pair needs about a quarter section (160 acres) of mature forest to raise their young. The nesting hole is excavated in a dead tree at least 12 inches in diameter and usually with a broken top. The wood must be decaying, but not yet spongy to touch. Such trees usually are at least 80 years of age and increasingly hard to find in forests managed for "maximum yields" of timber, pulp, and firewood.

Ironically, whereas the birds are becoming scarce in many traditional hardwood bottomlands managed by foresters or mismanaged by the U.S. Army Corps of Engineers, pileated woodpeckers seem to be thriving in bottomland parks surrounded by urban development. The Christmas Bird Count in the District of Columbia, for example, continues to turn up remarkable numbers of pileated woodpeckers. It's sad this species' larger cousin, the ivorybill, was unable to make a comparable adjustment to man's obsessive cleaning of the bottomland wilderness.

GILA WOODPECKER

Melanerpes uropygialis

Date of Sighting

Location of Sighting

Notes

NORTHERN FLICKER

Colaptes auratus

Date of Sighting

Location of Sighting

Notes

GOLDEN-FRONTED WOODPECKER
aurifrons

Date of Sighting

Location of Sighting

Notes

RED-BELLIED WOODPECKER
Melanerpes carolinus

Date of Sighting

Location of Sighting

Notes

WHITE-HEADED WOODPECKER
Picoides albolarvatus

Date of Sighting

Location of Sighting

Notes

LEWIS' WOODPECKER
Melanerpes lewis

Date of Sighting

Location of Sighting

Notes

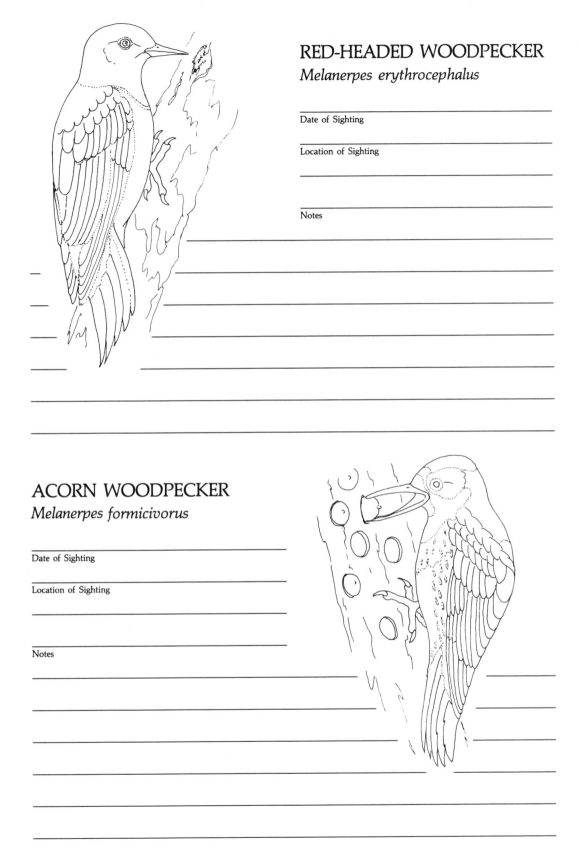

RED-HEADED WOODPECKER
Melanerpes erythrocephalus

Date of Sighting

Location of Sighting

Notes

ACORN WOODPECKER
Melanerpes formicivorus

Date of Sighting

Location of Sighting

Notes

YELLOW-BELLIED SAPSUCKER
Sphyrapicus varius

Date of Sighting

Location of Sighting

Notes

RED-NAPED SAPSUCKER
Sphyrapicus nuchalis

Date of Sighting

Location of Sighting

Notes

WILLIAMSON'S SAPSUCKER.
Sphyrapicus thyroideus

Date of Sighting

Location of Sighting

Notes

RED-BREASTED SAPSUCKER
Sphyrapicus ruber

Date of Sighting

Location of Sighting

Notes

THREE-TOED WOODPECKER
Picoides tridactylus

Date of Sighting

Location of Sighting

Notes

BLACK-BACKED WOODPECKER
Picoides arcticus

Date of Sighting

Location of Sighting

Notes

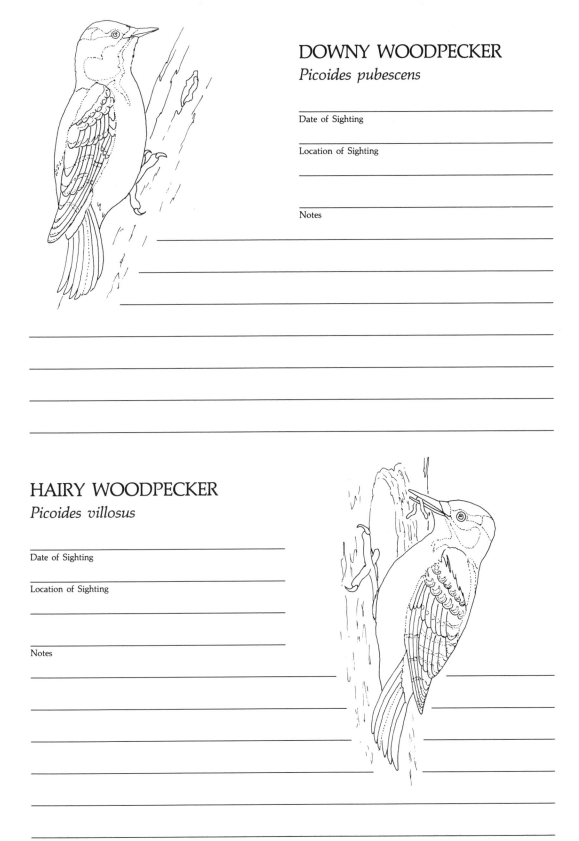

DOWNY WOODPECKER
Picoides pubescens

Date of Sighting

Location of Sighting

Notes

HAIRY WOODPECKER
Picoides villosus

Date of Sighting

Location of Sighting

Notes

NUTTALL'S WOODPECKER
Picoides nuttallii

Date of Sighting

Location of Sighting

Notes

STRICKLAND'S WOODPECKER
Picoides stricklandi

Date of Sighting

Location of Sighting

Notes

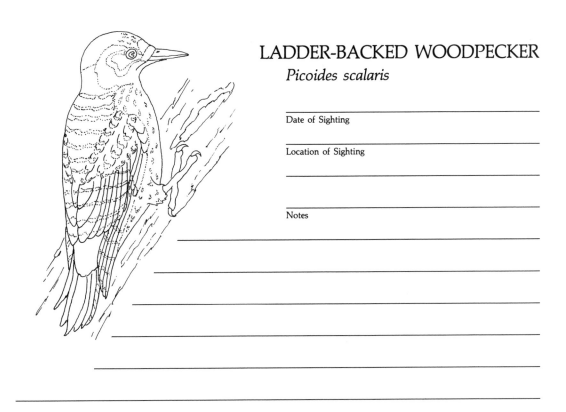

LADDER-BACKED WOODPECKER
Picoides scalaris

Date of Sighting

Location of Sighting

Notes

RED-COCKADED WOODPECKER
Picoides borealis

Date of Sighting

Location of Sighting

Notes

PILEATED WOODPECKER
Dryocopus pileatus

Date of Sighting

Location of Sighting

Notes

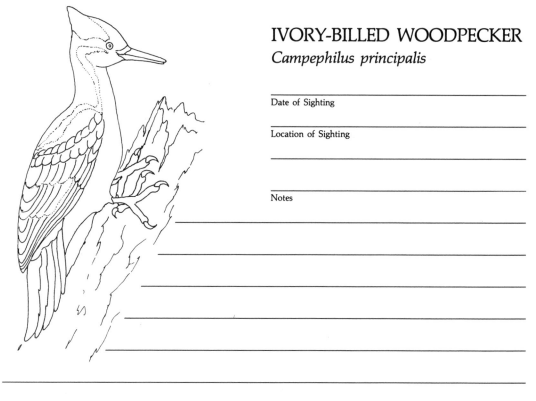

IVORY-BILLED WOODPECKER
Campephilus principalis

Date of Sighting

Location of Sighting

Notes

TYRANT FLYCATCHERS
(TYRANNIDAE)

Tyrant FLYCATCHERS

This Family has what amounts to "military bearing." Tyrant flycatchers appear to perch at attention. Their erect posture is coupled in many species with quick wing-flickers and tail-snappings, reminiscent of Marine officers slapping swagger-sticks against starched trouser legs.

This Family comes to us from the tropics and subtropics, and several of the species that visit North America seem to flaunt their exotic origins, elegant designs and colors. I was miles from anywhere in Oklahoma, driving across country with a college classmate, when I saw my first scissor-tailed flycatcher. My classmate was singularly unimpressed and wanted to drive on, but the car was mine, and I took the keys with me before running off across the field to get a closer look at this astonishing bird.

Yet even less startling members of the Family command attention. An eastern kingbird sat on a plant marker in our lower yard and allowed my family to sit in our car in the driveway and watch the bird feed on flying insects only a short distance away. Its proud demeanor captivated our attention for more than a quarter-hour before the business of life forced us to move on.

Then there were the two eastern phoebes that turned up in the woods behind my house during our local Christmas Bird Count. My companion that morning was crest-fallen that I'd spotted the birds first, because he needed a "Virginia phoebe" for his States' List.

"It's all right," I told him. "There are two of them. Why don't you take one?"

"May I?" he rhapsodized.

That evening during the tally, I reported one phoebe and he reported the other.

Eastern phoebes played an important role in early birding history. Although waterfowl had been banded by British royalty as far back as Charles II's seventeenth-century reign, John James Audubon became the first known American bird-bander when he wrapped "silver threads" around the legs of a brood of young phoebes with the hope of seeing one or more of them return the following year. Much to his delight, two of his banded birds returned and built their nests just up the creek from where they'd been reared.

GRAY KINGBIRD
Tyrannus dominicensis

Date of Sighting

Location of Sighting

Notes

EASTERN KINGBIRD
Tyrannus tyrannus

Date of Sighting

Location of Sighting

Notes

WESTERN KINGBIRD
Tyrannus verticalis

Date of Sighting

Location of Sighting

Notes

THICK-BILLED KINGBIRD
Tyrannus crassirostris

Date of Sighting

Location of Sighting

Notes

COUCH'S KINGBIRD
Tyrannus couchii

Date of Sighting

Location of Sighting

Notes

SCISSOR-TAILED FLYCATCHER
Tyrannus forficatus

Date of Sighting

Location of Sighting

Notes

CASSIN'S KINGBIRD
Tyrannus vociferans

Date of Sighting

Location of Sighting

Notes

TROPICAL KINGBIRD
Tyrannus melancholicus

Date of Sighting

Location of Sighting

Notes

GREAT KISKADEE
Pitangus sulphuratus

Date of Sighting

Location of Sighting

Notes

SULPHUR-BELLIED FLYCATCHER
Myiodynastes luteiventris

Date of Sighting

Location of Sighting

Notes

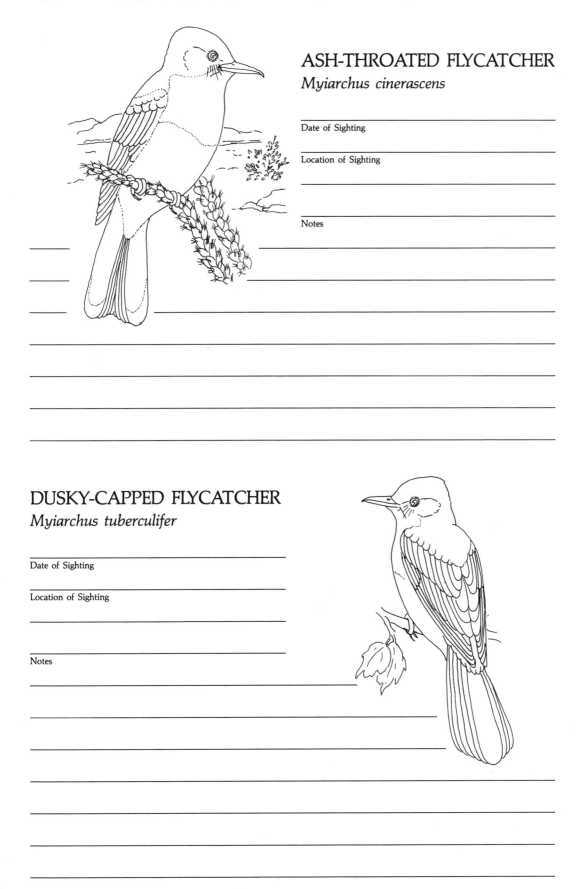

ASH-THROATED FLYCATCHER
Myiarchus cinerascens

Date of Sighting

Location of Sighting

Notes

DUSKY-CAPPED FLYCATCHER
Myiarchus tuberculifer

Date of Sighting

Location of Sighting

Notes

GREAT CRESTED FLYCATCHER
Myiarchus crinitus

Date of Sighting

Location of Sighting

Notes

BROWN-CRESTED FLYCATCHER
Myiarchus tyrannulus

Date of Sighting

Location of Sighting

Notes

OLIVE-SIDED FLYCATCHER
Contopus borealis

Date of Sighting

Location of Sighting

Notes

GREATER PEWEE
Contopus pertinax

Date of Sighting

Location of Sighting

Notes

WESTERN WOOD-PEWEE

Contopus sordidulus

Date of Sighting

Location of Sighting

Notes

EASTERN WOOD-PEWEE

Contopus virens

Date of Sighting

Location of Sighting

Notes

SAY'S PHOEBE
Sayornis saya

Date of Sighting

Location of Sighting

Notes

EASTERN PHOEBE
Sayornis phoebe

Date of Sighting

Location of Sighting

Notes

BLACK PHOEBE
Sayornis nigricans

Date of Sighting

Location of Sighting

Notes

VERMILLION FLYCATCHER
Pyrocephalus rubinus

Date of Sighting

Location of Sighting

Notes

GRAY FLYCATCHER
Empidonax wrightii

Date of Sighting

Location of Sighting

Notes

DUSKY FLYCATCHER
Empidonax oberholseri

Date of Sighting

Location of Sighting

Notes

HAMMOND'S FLYCATCHER
Empidonax hammondii

Date of Sighting

Location of Sighting

Notes

LEAST FLYCATCHER
Empidonax minimus

Date of Sighting

Location of Sighting

Notes

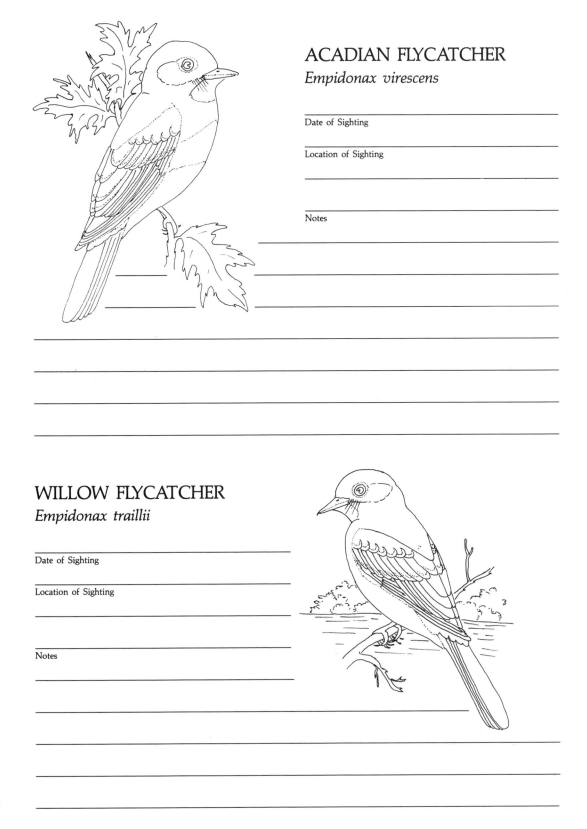

ACADIAN FLYCATCHER
Empidonax virescens

Date of Sighting

Location of Sighting

Notes

WILLOW FLYCATCHER
Empidonax traillii

Date of Sighting

Location of Sighting

Notes

ALDER FLYCATCHER
Empidonax alnorum

Date of Sighting

Location of Sighting

Notes

YELLOW-BELLIED FLYCATCHER
Empidonax flaviventris

Date of Sighting

Location of Sighting

Notes

WESTERN FLYCATCHER
Empidonax difficilis

Date of Sighting

Location of Sighting

Notes

BUFF-BREASTED FLYCATCHER
Empidonax fulvifrons

Date of Sighting

Location of Sighting

Notes

NORTHERN BEARDLESS-TYRANNULET
Camptostoma imberbe

Date of Sighting

Location of Sighting

Notes

ROSE-THROATED BECARD
Pachyramphus aglaiae

Date of Sighting

Location of Sighting

Notes

LARKS
(ALAUDIDAE)

Larks

It seems unfair to meadowlarks that they should be classified with blackbirds and grackles, for meadowlarks have many of the same behavioral characteristics of true larks and certainly a clearer, more cheerful, and lark-like song than the grackle. Yet the horned lark is our only true lark, and even this species is shared with Europe where it's called the "shore lark." The lark Family, whose scientific name possibly derives from two Celtic words for "high" and "song," evolved in the Old World where Europe boasts nearly a dozen species and South Africa has two dozen, or roughly one-third the world's total.

HORNED LARK
Eremophila alpestris

Date of Sighting

Location of Sighting

Notes

EURASIAN SKYLARK
Alauda arvensis

Date of Sighting

Location of Sighting

Notes

SWALLOWS
(HIRUNDINIDAE)

Swallows

Some birds are so pretty to watch, so beneficial, and respond so readily to a helping hand, people become downright possessive of them. I met a Finnish gold miner living between the Yukon and Kuskokwin rivers in Alaska. He had the only sauna for thousands of square miles and a cliff swallow colony under the eaves of the makeshift building housing the sauna. Torval was proud of his steam room, but he was prouder still of *his* swallows and couldn't understand why they had to leave him in the fall.

"I'd feed them," he assured me.

In my own corner of North America, I put up bluebird boxes with the expectation that most will be occupied by tree swallows. I leave the garage door open all summer long so that barn swallows will build their nests on the joists inside. And I make war on starlings and house sparrows on behalf of a purple martin colony that has been using two 12-room aluminum houses next to our pond for over a decade. Some years the birds are late or few in number, and I wonder about the hazards and hardships of their migration to and from South America. That such vulgar species as house sparrows and starlings can be so uppity in the presence of their avian superiors stirs possessive feelings in me akin to Torval's, even though I know I must share my elegant guests with other admirers thousands of miles away.

CAVE SWALLOW
Hirundo fulva

Date of Sighting

Location of Sighting

Notes

BARN SWALLOW
Hirundo rustica

Date of Sighting

Location of Sighting

Notes

TREE SWALLOW
Tachycineta bicolor

Date of Sighting

Location of Sighting

Notes

VIOLET-GREEN SWALLOW
Tachycineta thalassina

Date of Sighting

Location of Sighting

Notes

PURPLE MARTIN
Progne subis

Date of Sighting

Location of Sighting

Notes

BANK SWALLOW
Riparia riparia

Date of Sighting

Location of Sighting

Notes

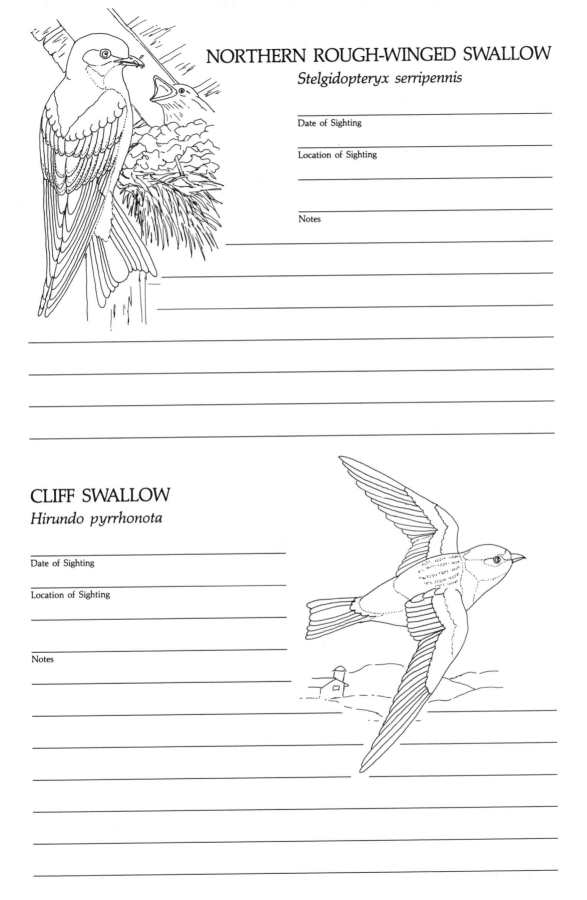

NORTHERN ROUGH-WINGED SWALLOW
Stelgidopteryx serripennis

Date of Sighting

Location of Sighting

Notes

CLIFF SWALLOW
Hirundo pyrrhonota

Date of Sighting

Location of Sighting

Notes

JAYS, CROWS, MAGPIES

(CORVIDAE)

JAYS, CROWS MAGPIES

This Family is like those kids we knew in school who took advantage of others but did it with such chutzpah, they earned our grudging admiration even though we never liked them very much. Such creatures are not content with stealing from others; they raise a ruckus over any competition as well. In the case of Corvidae, this competition is perceived to include hawks, owls, foxes, cats, and even innocent birders.

Although crows eat many insect pests and ravens clean up considerable carrion, there is no disguising the fact this Family works as much havoc among other birds and small mammals as bonafide raptors. Jays are particularly stealthy while doing the rounds of the neighborhood—taking the eggs of those birds too large to consume as nestlings, but preferring to wait for warblers to hatch. The bluejay may then do an excellent immitation of a red-shouldered or red-tailed hawk, as though trying to shift the blame for its nefarious deed onto another, more forthright predator.

Crows coined the term *forage*. They'll methodically patrol highways at dawn, looking for fresh road kills, and I once observed a line of fish crows undulating across a Virginia salt marsh. Periodic-

ally, one of the birds would drop into the grass to plunder a clapper rail or blackduck nest. The others waited for their comrade to finish. When the satisfied bandit rose into the air, the undulating line reformed and continued on its wanton way.

The Corvidae evolved in the Old World. None are native to South America, but over 40 species and subspecies (including European strays) have been found on this continent north of Mexico. Yet as habitats are altered, so are the prospects for birds living there. Half a century ago, the common crow was reckoned to be one of the most abundant birds in North America. Its numbers were expected to increase as even more marginal agricultural lands were cleared and planted to grain. However, the woodlots the birds need for roosting and nesting were also cleared, and vast monocultural fields replaced traditional farming habitats. Birds better able to make their homes in scanty windbreaks and hedgerows—blackbirds, grackles and mourning dove—gradually became an even more common sight in rural America than that of crows reconnoitering autumnal fields.

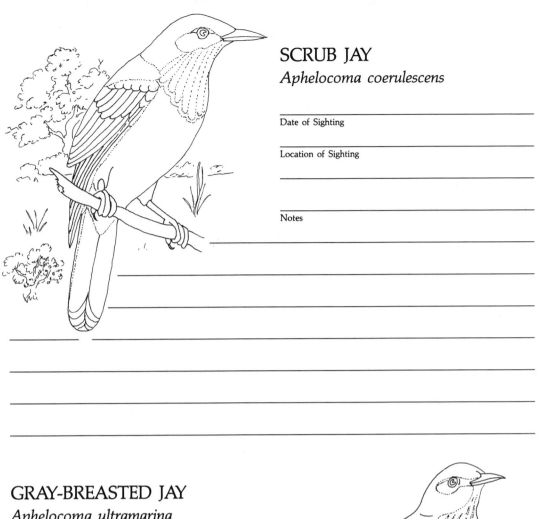

SCRUB JAY
Aphelocoma coerulescens

Date of Sighting

Location of Sighting

Notes

GRAY-BREASTED JAY
Aphelocoma ultramarina

Date of Sighting

Location of Sighting

Notes

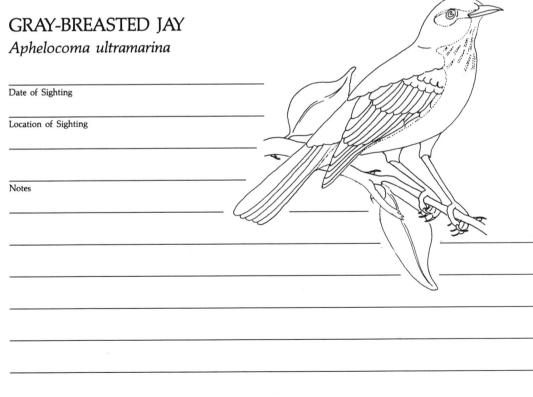

PINYON JAY
Gymnorhinus cyanocephalus

Date of Sighting

Location of Sighting

Notes

BLUE JAY
Cyanocitta cristata

Date of Sighting

Location of Sighting

Notes

STELLER'S JAY
Cyanocitta stelleri

Date of Sighting

Location of Sighting

Notes

GRAY JAY
Perisoreus canadensis

Date of Sighting

Location of Sighting

Notes

CLARK'S NUTCRACKER
Nucifraga columbiana

Date of Sighting _____

Location of Sighting _____

_____

_____

Notes

_____

_____

_____

_____

_____

_____

_____

BROWN JAY
Cyanocorax morio

Date of Sighting _____

Location of Sighting _____

_____

_____

Notes

_____

_____

_____

_____

_____

_____

GREEN JAY
Cyanocorax yncas

Date of Sighting

Location of Sighting

Notes

BLACK-BILLED MAGPIE
Pica pica

Date of Sighting

Location of Sighting

Notes

YELLOW-BILLED MAGPIE
Pica nuttalli

Date of Sighting

Location of Sighting

Notes

AMERICAN CROW
Corvus brachyrhynchos

Date of Sighting

Location of Sighting

Notes

NORTHWESTERN CROW
Corvus caurinus

Date of Sighting

Location of Sighting

Notes

FISH CROW
Corvus ossifragus

Date of Sighting

Location of Sighting

Notes

CHIHUAHUAN RAVEN
Corvus cryptoleucus

Date of Sighting

Location of Sighting

Notes

COMMON RAVEN
Corvus corax

Date of Sighting

Location of Sighting

Notes

WRENTIT
(MUSCICAPIDAE)

Wrentit

This is one of those birds Easterners must learn the song of if they hope to add the species to their life lists. The scientific name *Chamaea* refers to the wrentit's preference for the ground, particularly under California chapparal and in coniferous brush. They're next to impossible to flush into view. The National Geographic Society's bird guide says that "wrentits are often heard before they are seen." The truth is wrentits are more often heard, period. The males sing year-round a pitting-trilling call which should be certified by an expert birder so you can identify the sound next time on your own.

WRENTIT
Chamaea fasciata

Date of Sighting

Location of Sighting

Notes

TITMICE AND CHICKADEES

(PARIDAE)

TITMICE AND CHICKADEES

All of us admire spunkiness, and no bird better embodies that concept than those in this Family. Capture a chickadee in a mist-net for banding, and the feisty little guy will rap a fierce tatoo on your thumbnail—or try to nip out a plug of flesh. Let him go, and he'll fly up into a tree and scold you for bothering him in the first place.

My favorite chickadee anecdote comes courtesy of Les Line, editor of *Audubon* magazine. One morning in his bow-hunting youth, he spotted a deer meandering down a trail toward his stand. By the time the animal was directly below him, Les was trembling with excitement. He slowly drew back the bow string, held his breath—when suddenly a small bird landed plumb on the arrow: chick-a-dee-dee-dee it proclaimed. The arrow, the bird, and the deer all went in different directions.

TUFTED TITMOUSE
Parus bicolor

Date of Sighting

Location of Sighting

Notes

PLAIN TITMOUSE
Parus inornatus

Date of Sighting

Location of Sighting

Notes

BRIDLED TITMOUSE
Parus wollweberi

Date of Sighting

Location of Sighting

Notes

BLACK-CAPPED CHICKADEE
Parus atricapillus

Date of Sighting

Location of Sighting

Notes

CAROLINA CHICKADEE
Parus carolinensis

Date of Sighting

Location of Sighting

Notes

MEXICAN CHICKADEE
Parus sclateri

Date of Sighting

Location of Sighting

Notes

MOUNTAIN CHICKADEE
Parus gambeli

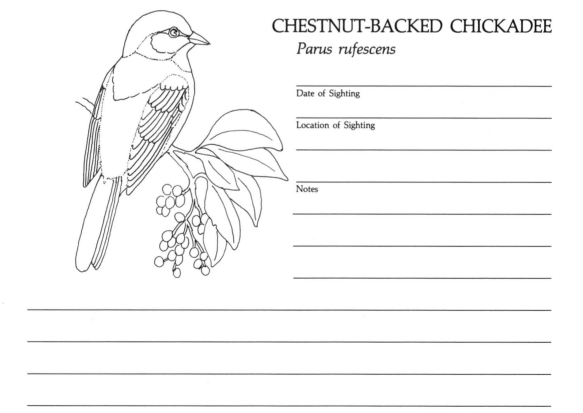

Date of Sighting

Location of Sighting

Notes

CHESTNUT-BACKED CHICKADEE
Parus rufescens

Date of Sighting

Location of Sighting

Notes

SIBERIAN TIT

Parus cinctus

Date of Sighting

Location of Sighting

Notes

BOREAL CHICKADEE

Parus hudsonicus

Date of Sighting

Location of Sighting

Notes

VERDINS
(REMIZIDAE)

Verdins

The scientific name for this species means the "gold" or "yellow-head titmouse." That sums it up, for where the pine and oak habitat of true titmice and chickadees fades into the mesquite scrub of the Southwest, you'll find the verdin.

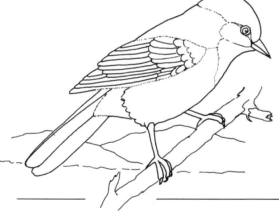

VERDIN
Auriparus flaviceps

Date of Sighting

Location of Sighting

Notes

BUSHTITS
(AEGITHALIDAE)

Bushtits

On arriving in Seattle to make a speech on marine wildlife a number of years ago, I happened to remark to my host, a physician and fellow naturalist, that I'd never seen the pendant nest of a bushtit. "Oh, I'll take care of that!" he said with enthusiastic pride. And when we got to his home, there, indeed, was a bushtit nest hanging conveniently by the front window so I could sit and watch the birds while having tea and recuperating from my journey.

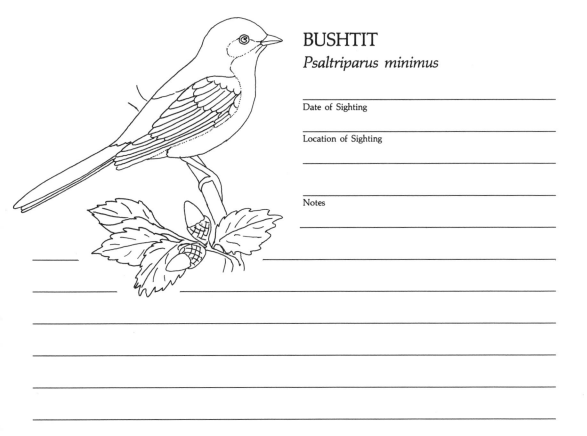

BUSHTIT
Psaltriparus minimus

Date of Sighting

Location of Sighting

Notes

CREEPERS
(CERTHIIDAE)

CREEPERS

The first one of these I saw as a youngster, I mistook for a mouse when it seemed to scamper from near the forest floor up and around the back of a tree. When I pushed through the overhanging branches to investigate, imagine my surprise when my mystery mouse flew away!

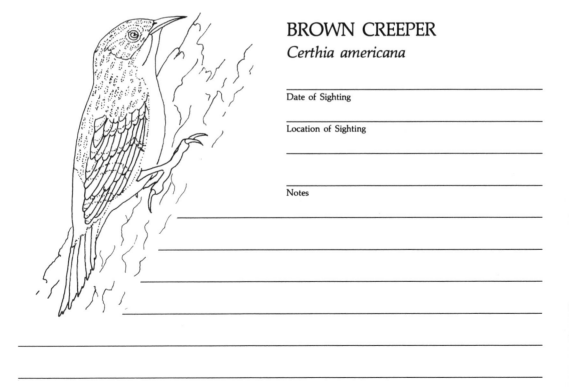

BROWN CREEPER
Certhia americana

Date of Sighting

Location of Sighting

Notes

NUTHATCHES
(SITTIDAE)

Nuthatches

Suburban suet cakes and bird feeders have been kind to this Family, helping it not only to hold its own in the face of enormous and ongoing environmental changes, but even enabling the red-breasted species to expand its range.

The susceptibility of many small birds, but especially red-breasted nuthatches, to recorded screech owl sounds has stirred a controversy among birders as to the ethics of using tape recorders to lure birds. The concern is not only whether such recordings are reducing the value of the mobbing behavior of small birds confronting real owls, but whether troupes of birders who spend much time provoking local populations of chickadees and nuthatches with screech owl sounds are not also keeping the little birds from finding sufficient food to fuel their highly energetic bodies. I personally doubt there is much problem yet, but as in all controversies concerning people and wildlife, molehills become mountains as our human population continues to swell.

PYGMY NUTHATCH
Sitta pygmaea

Date of Sighting

Location of Sighting

Notes

BROWN-HEADED NUTHATCH
Sitta pusilla

Date of Sighting

Location of Sighting

Notes

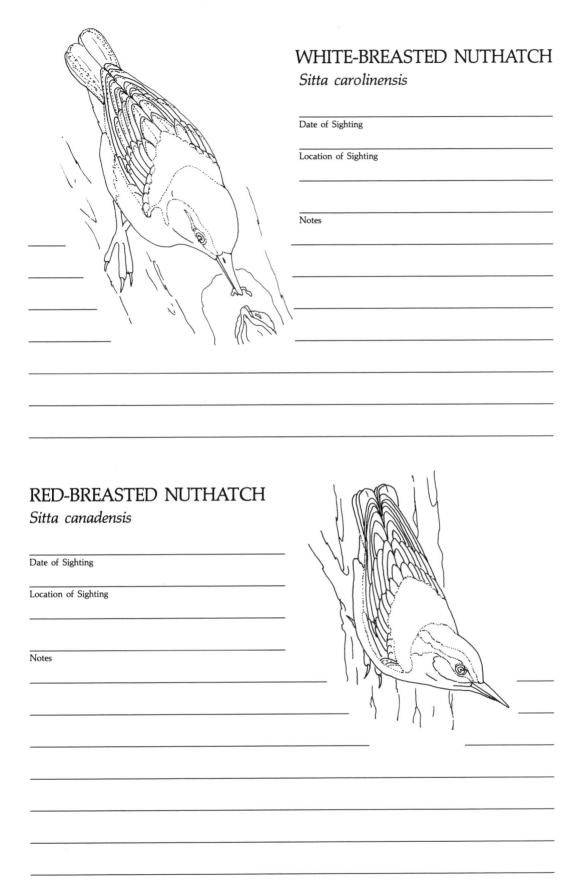

WHITE-BREASTED NUTHATCH
Sitta carolinensis

Date of Sighting

Location of Sighting

Notes

RED-BREASTED NUTHATCH
Sitta canadensis

Date of Sighting

Location of Sighting

Notes

WRENS
(TROGLODYTIDAE)

Wrens

In January 1969, I went to Paris as a member of the negotiating team to end the war in Vietnam. We worked six-day weeks. I had to be at the American Embassy each morning before dawn, and I often stayed until nine at night. Many days passed without my seeing even the light of day, much less taking a walk in a park. I missed seeing birds and was pleased one Sunday afternoon to spy a familiar winter wren in the shrubbery in front of the UNESCO building. Wanting to know its French name, I asked a friend who told me "troglodyte." I was puzzled. *Troglodyte* means "cave dweller" in Greek, and the term is usually applied to primitive people living in caves. It struck me as odd that the French would link the wren with prototypical man. On the

other hand, considering the wren's still bewildering capacity to produce high volumes of mellifluous sound from such tiny but hyperactive bodies, the bird is like certain small people who compensate for their diminutive size by being extremely busy and extremely loud.

No other birds live so familiarly with rural man than wrens. Consequently no birds have had so many stories and legends told about them. One dating back to at least Roman times concerns a contest between the birds to select a ruler. The species able to ascend the highest would win. The eagle soared far above his competitors and was about to scream his victory when a series of triumphant trills came from a tiny wren perched on the eagle's back.

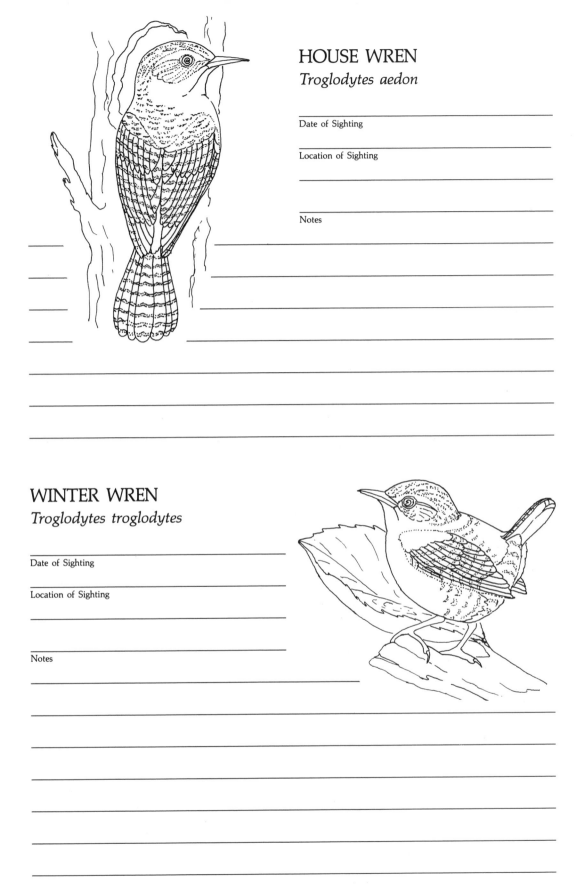

HOUSE WREN
Troglodytes aedon

Date of Sighting

Location of Sighting

Notes

WINTER WREN
Troglodytes troglodytes

Date of Sighting

Location of Sighting

Notes

CAROLINA WREN
Thryothorus ludovicianus

Date of Sighting

Location of Sighting

Notes

BEWICK'S WREN
Thryomanes bewickii

Date of Sighting

Location of Sighting

Notes

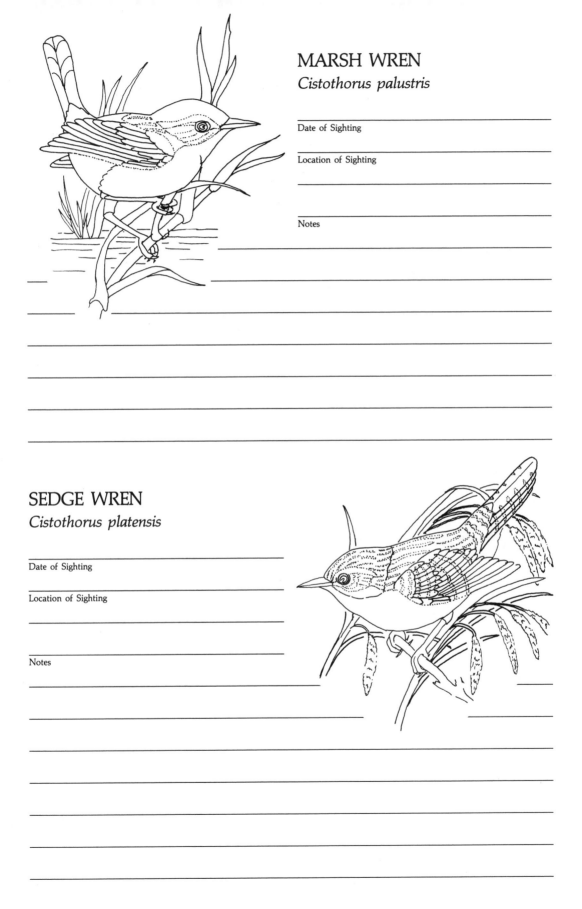

MARSH WREN
Cistothorus palustris

Date of Sighting

Location of Sighting

Notes

SEDGE WREN
Cistothorus platensis

Date of Sighting

Location of Sighting

Notes

CANYON WREN
Catherpes mexicanus

Date of Sighting

Location of Sighting

Notes

ROCK WREN
Salpinctes obsoletus

Date of Sighting

Location of Sighting

Notes

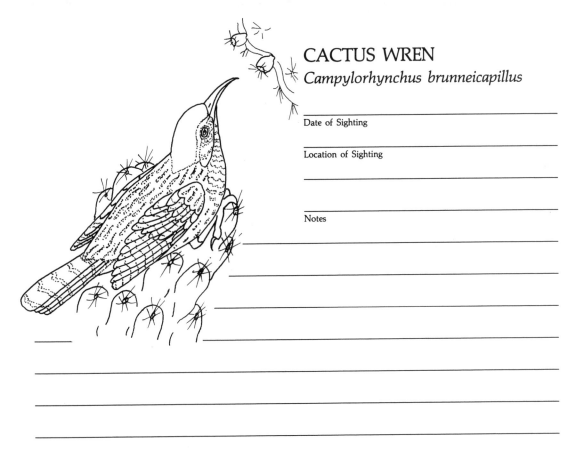

CACTUS WREN
Campylorhynchus brunneicapillus

Date of Sighting

Location of Sighting

Notes

THRUSHES
(MUSCICAPIDAE)

THRUSHES

When I was a child, I was fascinated by thrushes for the not very admirable reason that I though the best known of them, the robin, had a scatological scientific name. *Turdus* was what I imagined the Romans called fecal matter. I assumed the allusion was to the robin's dun-colored back, and I giggled over the image of a "migrating turd." Only gradually did I come to understand that the word *turdus* meant something very different in Latin than its Anglo-Saxon sound-alike.

This is one Family which every conscientious birder should spend some time learning its songs. Many species inhabit shadowy hardwood forests where the birds are difficult to spot, or they migrate at night when the only evidence of their passage wafts ethereally from the starlit heavens above. The robin sings as beautifully as any of the other thrushes, but because it's commonly heard, it's unappreciated.

ARCTIC WARBLER
Phylloscopus borealis

Date of Sighting

Location of Sighting

Notes

GOLDEN-CROWNED KINGLET
Regulus satrapa

Date of Sighting

Location of Sighting

Notes

RUBY-CROWNED KINGLET
Regulus calendula

Date of Sighting

Location of Sighting

Notes

BLUE-GRAY GNATCATCHER
Polioptila caerulea

Date of Sighting

Location of Sighting

Notes

BLACK-TAILED GNATCATCHER
Polioptila melanura

Date of Sighting

Location of Sighting

Notes

EASTERN BLUEBIRD
Sialia sialis

Date of Sighting

Location of Sighting

Notes

WESTERN BLUEBIRD

Sialia mexicana

Date of Sighting

Location of Sighting

Notes

MOUNTAIN BLUEBIRD

Sialia currucoides

Date of Sighting

Location of Sighting

Notes

TOWNSEND'S SOLITAIRE
Myadestes townsendi

Date of Sighting

Location of Sighting

Notes

WOOD THRUSH
Hylocichla mustelina

Date of Sighting

Location of Sighting

Notes

VEERY
Catharus fuscescens

Date of Sighting _____

Location of Sighting _____

_____

Notes _____

_____

_____

_____

_____

_____

_____

_____

_____

SWAINSON'S THRUSH
Catharus ustulatus

Date of Sighting _____

Location of Sighting _____

_____

Notes _____

_____

_____

_____

_____

_____

_____

_____

296

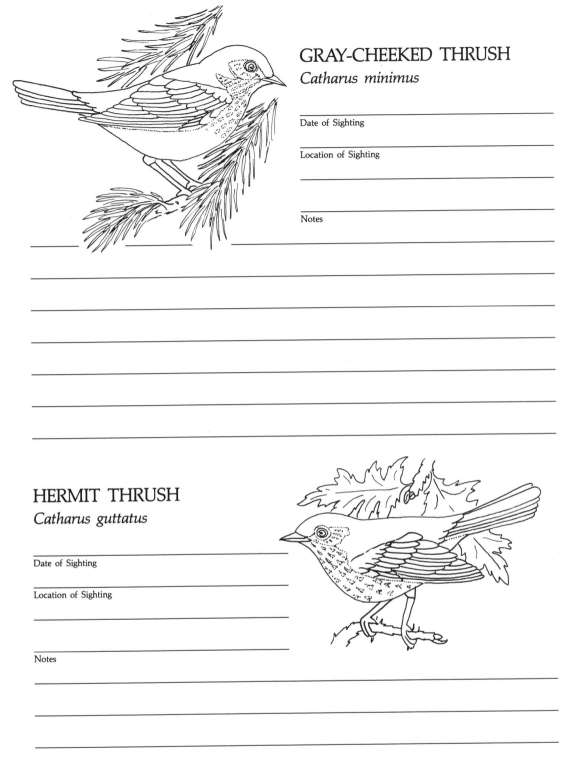

GRAY-CHEEKED THRUSH
Catharus minimus

Date of Sighting

Location of Sighting

Notes

HERMIT THRUSH
Catharus guttatus

Date of Sighting

Location of Sighting

Notes

VARIED THRUSH
Ixoreus naevius

Date of Sighting

Location of Sighting

Notes

AMERICAN ROBIN
Turdus Migratorius

Date of Sighting

Location of Sighting

Notes

NORTHERN WHEATEAR
Oenanthe oenanthe

Date of Sighting

Location of Sighting

Notes

BLUETHROAT
Luscinia svecica

Date of Sighting

Location of Sighting

Notes

SHRIKES
(LANIIDAE)

Shrikes

When I was a youngster, country people called these species "butcher-birds," which unintentionally tied rural venacular to scientific nomenclature since the Family name for shrikes means "butcher." In my walks around the fields (now mostly housing sub-divisions) behind the Lawrenceville School in New Jersey, I'd commonly find the evidence of shrikes, if not the birds themselves, impaled on the thorns of locust trees. Mostly I'd see insects stuck on the thorns. Only once do I recall seeing a mouse or vole impaled that way. When I learned that shrikes also eat small birds and reptiles as well as rodents, I decided shrikes must be like little boys at a dining table who "save" less desirable beets and brussel sprouts for last. At least, if I were a shrike, I'd prefer eating sparrows to crickets and grasshoppers!

The fierceness of this Family is awesome to behold. In January 1988, a northern shrike was caught in a Patuxent, Maryland mistnet, banded and released. However, it was quickly caught again and again as it persisted in attacking other birds struggling in the net. It was finally taken some distance away and released.

The shrike's compulsion to kill may explain accumulations of forgotten prey. Lacking talons, shrikes impale the birds or insects they've caught so the prey can be braced for easier rending. If a "butcher shop" is located in a fecund ecosystem, the shrike may be distracted from finishing one meal by the movements of other prey. This is especially true in the late summer when fields may be swarming with grasshoppers and crickets. By the time a shrike has caught and impaled all the larger insects in the vicinity of a thorn tree, he may have forgotten about some of those he started with.

During the first Wachapreague (Virginia) Christmas Bird Count, I spied a loggerhead strike in a hedge near the Chesapeake Bay. Because that shrike has been the only one of this declining species reported in all the Wachapreague counts since, I'd begun to doubt my recollection. Immature shrikes *do* resemble northern mockingbirds. Then I remembered the predatory brow and slightly hooked bill of what I saw and let the record stand.

LOGGERHEAD SHRIKE
Lanius ludovicianus

Date of Sighting

Location of Sighting

Notes

NORTHERN SHRIKE
Lanius excubitor

Date of Sighting

Location of Sighting

Notes

MIMIC THRUSHES
(MIMIDAE)

MIMIC THRUSHES

The songs of each mockingbird become a catalog of every other bird in that mocker's territory, and even a few that are not. Harry Armistead, a top-flight mimic in his own right, has heard mockingbirds imitate Virginia rail a good many leagues from the nearest Virginia rail habitat, and he heard another mocker duplicate the call of a chuck-will's-widow in suburban Philadelphia.

In the spring of 1978, two Smithsonian technicians visited my Virginia farm to collect bird specimens to replace the moth-eaten mounts in that institution's "Birds of the District of Columbia Region" exhibit. Even though I was familiar with the niche theory—that after an individual of a species is removed from a given ecosystem, another individual of that same species will soon replace it so long as the ecosystem itself hasn't been altered—I was curious to learn how well the theory would work with such highly competitive species as the catbird, mockingbird, and brown thrasher.

My wife, however, was not enthusiastic about having some of her favorite songbirds collected. She assumed most of the mayhem would occur far from the house and garden where a favorite mockingbird called "Caruso" held forth. Unfortunately, in the confusion of the afternoon, Caruso, alas, was also collected.

I tried to console Barbara with the thought that Caruso would have died of natural causes within a year or two, while now he has been immortalized for our son to see in the Natural History Museum for decades to come. Barbara was not persuaded.

The next spring, however, by which time the garden niche had probably gone through a couple of changings of the guard, Barbara rushed into my office one morning to announce that "Pavarotti" was a better singer than Caruso had been: Pavarotti could imitate ospreys!

Sure enough, when I ran outside to hear the latest chimney-top occupant, the mockingbird sang several local golden oldies—including cardinal, red-winged blackbird, white-throated sparrow, and bob-white quail—then did a remarkably accurate imitation of the osprey that comes each spring to fish in the pond next to our house.

Although multiflora rose hedges are now out of favor with state conservation agencies due to the ease with which birds propagate the thorny vines into pastures where they're not wanted, this plant is one reason the mockingbird has successfully pushed its range hundreds of miles north of where it was several decades ago. Besides providing protection from predators, multiflora rose produces rose-hips packed with calories the mockingbirds need in late winter.

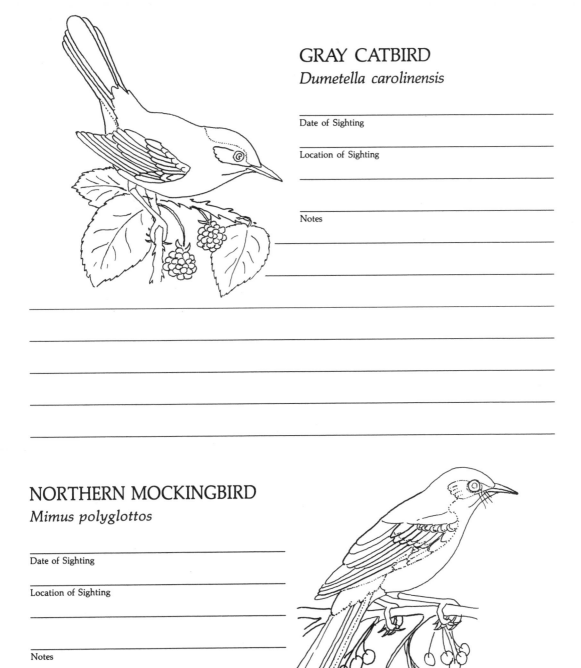

GRAY CATBIRD
Dumetella carolinensis

Date of Sighting

Location of Sighting

Notes

NORTHERN MOCKINGBIRD
Mimus polyglottos

Date of Sighting

Location of Sighting

Notes

SAGE THRASHER
Oreoscoptes montanus

Date of Sighting

Location of Sighting

Notes

BROWN THRASHER
Toxostoma rufum

Date of Sighting

Location of Sighting

Notes

LONG-BILLED THRASHER
Toxostoma longirostre

Date of Sighting

Location of Sighting

Notes

CURVE-BILLED THRASHER
Toxostoma curvirostre

Date of Sighting

Location of Sighting

Notes

BENDIRE'S THRASHER
Toxostoma bendirei

Date of Sighting

Location of Sighting

Notes

CRISSAL THRASHER
Toxostoma crissale

Date of Sighting

Location of Sighting

Notes

LE CONTE'S THRASHER
Toxostoma lecontei

Date of Sighting

Location of Sighting

Notes

CALIFORNIA THRASHER
Toxostoma redivivum

Date of Sighting

Location of Sighting

Notes

PIPITS AND WAGTAILS
(MOTACILLIDAE)

PIPITS AND WAGTAILS

The water pipit may have been especially created for Christmas Bird Counters, since this species is not often noted outside the context of a CBC, when it becomes a bonus for birding enumerators whose territories include bare winter fields or beaches. A little cross examination goes with the sighting: "Did you see the white outer feathers on the tail?" "Did the bird walk or hop?" "Did it wag its tail?" The questions are perfunctory since there's no mistaking a "wagtail" after you've seen one. But the litany appears to be the only way the water pipit gets much recognition. As for the rarer, secretive, and non-tail-wagging Sprague's pipit, "Where did you say you saw it?!"

WATER PIPIT
Anthus spinoletta

Date of Sighting

Location of Sighting

Notes

SPRAGUE'S PIPIT
Anthus spragueii

Date of Sighting

Location of Sighting

Notes

RED-THROATED PIPIT
Anthus cervinus

Date of Sighting

Location of Sighting

Notes

YELLOW WAGTAIL
Motacilla flava

Date of Sighting

Location of Sighting

Notes

DIPPERS
(CINCLIDAE)

Dippers

Everything about this bird is *neat*: its appearance, its bobbing behavior, its habitat. Show me a pristine western mountain stream, and I'll show you a dipper. Watching them has helped make memorable many pleasant, but unspectacular trout-fishing trips from New Mexico to Alaska. A dipper popping in and out of the water is as astonishing the hundreth time you see it as the first. Sometimes shy, other times tame, dippers always make you feel good about being where you are and doing what you're doing.

AMERICAN DIPPER
Cinclus mexicanus

Date of Sighting

Location of Sighting

Notes

WAXWINGS
(BOMBYCILLIDAE)

Waxwings

There's a battered red cedar about 250 years old standing in my front yard. Every spring a starling pair attempts to raise a family in a hole high on one side, and every year a blacksnake gets the young. A black cherry tree tries to grow from a crevice in the cedar, but each summer I cut it back. I sometimes wonder at the storms the cedar must have weathered and the events it must have witnessed.

That tree and I shared one especially memorable event. It was too early to be spring, but too late to be winter, when a huge flock of waxwings materialized one morning on the ancient tree and began stripping it of its lush crop of purple berries. The birds were so numerous that branches bent under their weight, and the litter of their feeding—both leafy debris and droppings—covered the ground below. It was enthralling to watch the feathered swarm churn and chatter its way through the foliage until there was not a berry left. Then the birds vanished as suddenly as they'd appeared.

BOHEMIAN WAXWING
Bombycilla garrulus

Date of Sighting

Location of Sighting

Notes

CEDAR WAXWING
Bombycilla cedrorum

Date of Sighting

Location of Sighting

Notes

SILKY FLYCATCHERS
(PTILOGONATIDAE)

Silky Flycatchers

When a bird's common name is the same as its scientific name, it suggests the species has never stirred the popular imagination. That's too bad, for phainopeplas are stirring little birds. Their name means "shining robe" in Greek, and the glossy soft plumage of the males has the quality of black velvet. This species also has a curious domestic life in which the males generally build the nests and incubate the eggs while the females help only in feeding the young.

PHAINOPEPLA
Phainopepla nitens

Date of Sighting
_____

Location of Sighting
_____

_____

Notes
_____

_____

_____

_____

_____

_____

_____

STARLINGS
(STURNIDAE)

Starlings

Had the sentimentalist who released the first starlings in New York City a century ago in order to bring all the birds of Shakespeare to the New World thought of Linnaeus' scientific name for this species, rather than just the English version, he might have decided not to do the terrible deed. The word *vulgar* has a double-meaning in Linnaeus' native Swedish as well as in the Latin he adopted. Like the word *common*, it suggests "aggressively unattractive" as well as "commonplace."

Although some recently published bird books have tried to put a bright face on the over-population of common starlings in North America by mentioning the many grubs and caterpillars these birds consume each year, the net effect of their introduction is still overwhelmingly negative—especially when we consider the many native cavity-nesting species they've usurped who would have otherwise eaten those same grubs, caterpillars and far, far more in the way of injurious insects.

One curious aspect of the hundreds of millions of starlings that now inhabit North America is that no entrepreneur has yet exploited their unprotected status to trap the birds and process them into some euphemistically-named hors d'oeuvre. They are flavorful as well as good protein, and I once served them as "sora rail" to eight appreciative dinner guests, most of whom weren't even angry with me after I told them they'd just eaten (and raved about) *Sturnus vulgaris.*

Two other attributes of this species: they are under-rated mimics, and their white-tipped fall feathers provide the basis of an unusual, but effective wet fly for trout fishing.

EUROPEAN STARLING
Sturnus vulgaris

Date of Sighting

Location of Sighting

Notes

VIREOS
(VIREONIDAE)

Vireos

This Family and the next includes uniquely New World songsters that evolved in South America and from which a relatively small number of species (12 out of 75 in the case of vireos) pioneered north to breed and, in a few cases, to live out their entire life cycles. Insectivores that evolved in the lush Amazonian watershed, vireos prefer similarly forested bottomlands in North America where our temperate climate produces great spring hatches of soft-bodied insects.

Some songbirds migrating from South America occasionally arrive too early and suffer consequences in the form of late winter storms. Vireos avoid this by always being the last to arrive—after the pecans and butternuts are fully leafed— to be here when the woods are fully alive with invertebrate prey. Most are tireless singers, especially the red-eyes, which will continue singing on the hottest August afternoons after all the other birds have fallen silent.

WHITE-EYED VIREO
Vireo griseus

Date of Sighting

Location of Sighting

Notes

BLACK-CAPED VIREO
Vireo atricapillus

Date of Sighting

Location of Sighting

Notes

HUTTON'S VIREO
Vireo huttoni

Date of Sighting

Location of Sighting

Notes

GRAY VIREO
Vireo vicinior

Date of Sighting

Location of Sighting

Notes

SOLITARY VIREO
Vireo solitarius

Date of Sighting

Location of Sighting

Notes

RED-EYED VIREO
Vireo olivaceus

Date of Sighting

Location of Sighting

Notes

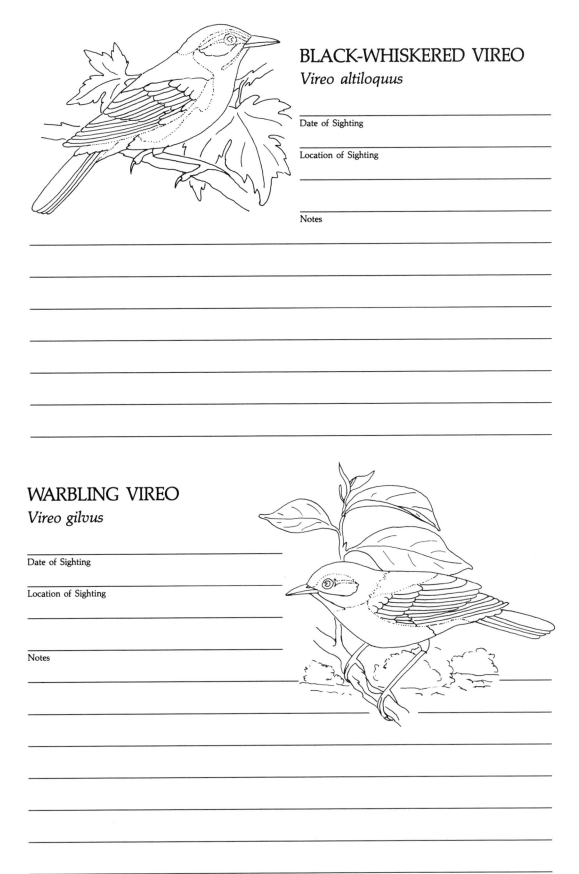

BLACK-WHISKERED VIREO
Vireo altiloquus

Date of Sighting

Location of Sighting

Notes

WARBLING VIREO
Vireo gilvus

Date of Sighting

Location of Sighting

Notes

YELLOW-THROATED VIREO
Vireo flavifrons

Date of Sighting

Location of Sighting

Notes

BELL'S VIREO
Vireo bellii

Date of Sighting

Location of Sighting

Notes

PHILADELPHIA VIREO
philadelphicus

Date of Sighting

Location of Sighting

Notes

WARBLERS AND SPARROWS

(EMBERIZIDAE)

Warblers and Sparrows

In its variety of species and numbers of individuals, this is the most important bird family in North America. One genus of warblers alone, *Dendroica*, includes more species than any other genus of birds that visits or lives on this continent.

The colorful warblers, buntings, and grosbeaks provide proof of their tropical origins when they migrate south each autumn, most of them to Central and South America. Yet even our resident cardinals and rufous-sided towhees give evidence of their tropical antecedents with bright colors and patterns more characteristic of equatorial rain forests than the temperate deciduous forest edges where they live today.

The huge size of this Family results from several scientific reclassifications over the past half century. The wood warblers were once listed in one Family and the blackbirds and orioles in another. The Emberizidae—including towhees, sparrows, longspurs and snow buntings—were once considered to be a subFamily of the finches (Fringillidae).

Although taxonomic lumpers have temporarily triumphed over the splitters, scientific classification seems to be as subject to pendulum swings of opinion as any other form of intellectual activity. Speaking as an interested by-stander, I'd like to see blackbirds and orioles separated from warblers, for the only characteristic they seem to have in common is an inclination to retire each fall toward the land of their ancestors. Only the bobolink among blackbirds still makes the incredible journey each year between southern Canada and northern Argentina.

The principal advantage of having so many different birds with so many different niches is that there's bound to be at least one species in the family to stir a young person's birding interest. I was seven when I discovered an ovenbird nest directly below one of the sunporch windows of my family's house in Forest Hills Gardens, Long Island. I looked up my discovery in the National Geographic Society's old, 2-volume *Book of Birds.* I was thrilled by an editorial implication that even children could make contributions to science, for the essence of intellectual discipline is mere curiosity.

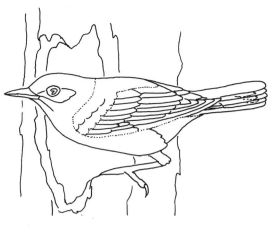

PROTHONOTARY WARBLER
Protonotaria citrea

Date of Sighting

Location of Sighting

Notes

BLUE-WINGED WARBLER
Vermivora pinus

Date of Sighting

Location of Sighting

Notes

GOLDEN-WINGED WARBLER
Vermivora chrysoptera

Date of Sighting

Location of Sighting

Notes

TENNESSEE WARBLER
Vermivora peregrina

Date of Sighting

Location of Sighting

Notes

LUCY'S WARBLER
Vermivora luciae

Date of Sighting

Location of Sighting

Notes

NASHVILLE WARBLER
Vermivora ruficapilla

Date of Sighting

Location of Sighting

Notes

BACHMAN'S WARBLER
Vermivora bachmanii

Date of Sighting

Location of Sighting

Notes

ORANGE-CROWNED WARBLER
Vermivora celata

Date of Sighting

Location of Sighting

Notes

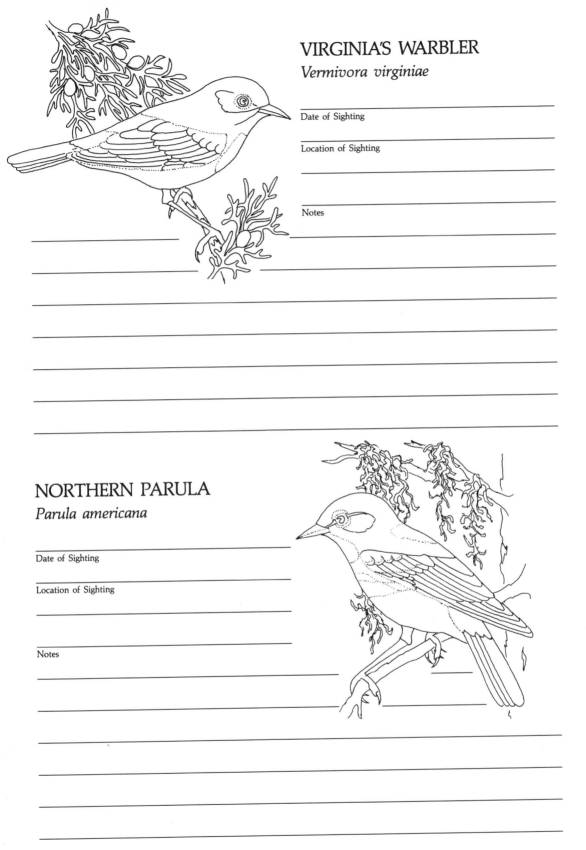

VIRGINIA'S WARBLER
Vermivora virginiae

Date of Sighting

Location of Sighting

Notes

NORTHERN PARULA
Parula americana

Date of Sighting

Location of Sighting

Notes

TROPICAL PARULA
Parula pitiayumi

Date of Sighting

Location of Sighting

Notes

BLACK-AND-WHITE WARBLER
Mniotilta varia

Date of Sighting

Location of Sighting

Notes

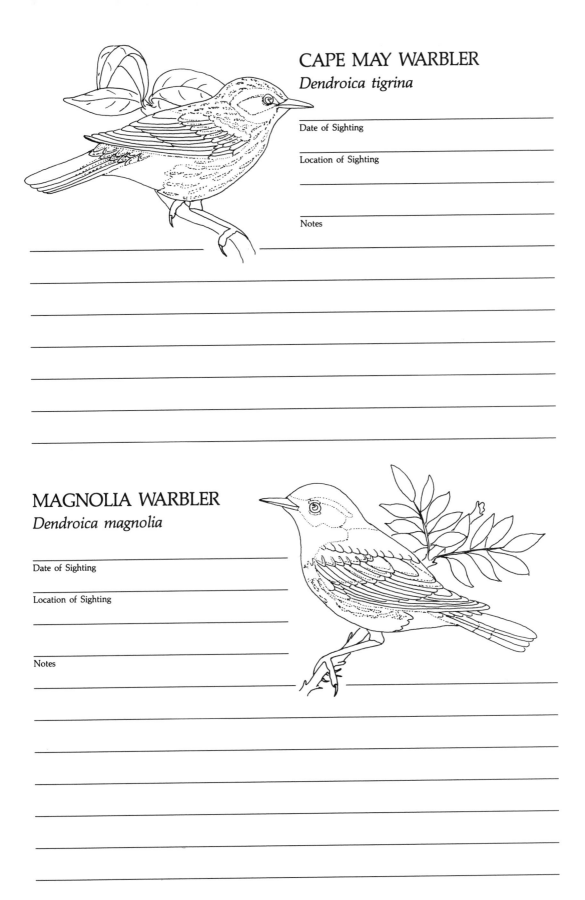

CAPE MAY WARBLER
Dendroica tigrina

Date of Sighting

Location of Sighting

Notes

MAGNOLIA WARBLER
Dendroica magnolia

Date of Sighting

Location of Sighting

Notes

BLACKBURNIAN WARBLER
Dendroica fusca

Date of Sighting

Location of Sighting

Notes

CHESTNUT-SIDED WARBLER
Dendroica pensylvanica

Date of Sighting

Location of Sighting

Notes

TOWNSEND'S WARBLER
Dendroica townsendi

Date of Sighting

Location of Sighting

Notes

HERMIT WARBLER
Dendroica occidentalis

Date of Sighting

Location of Sighting

Notes

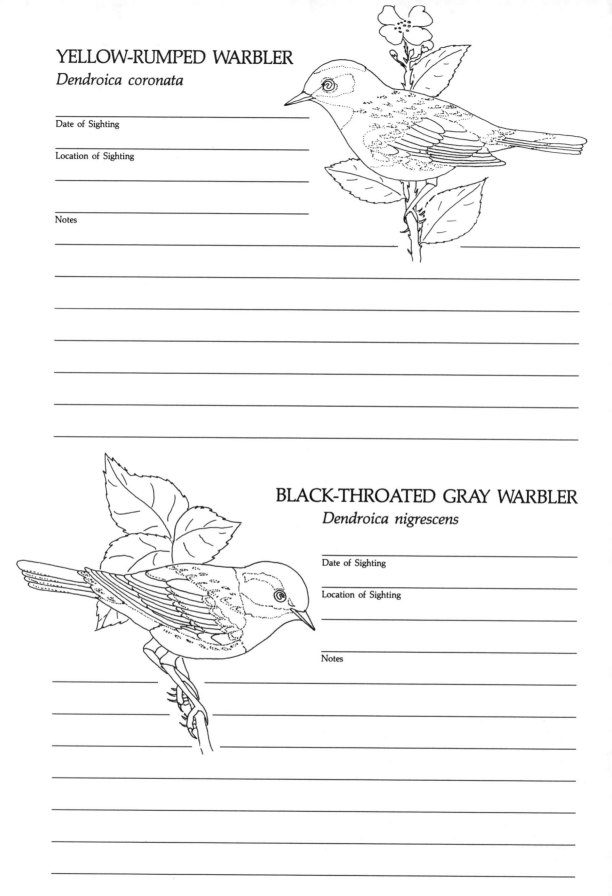

YELLOW-RUMPED WARBLER
Dendroica coronata

Date of Sighting

Location of Sighting

Notes

BLACK-THROATED GRAY WARBLER
Dendroica nigrescens

Date of Sighting

Location of Sighting

Notes

YELLOW-THROATED WARBLER
Dendroica dominica

Date of Sighting

Location of Sighting

Notes

GRACE'S WARBLER
Dendroica graciae

Date of Sighting

Location of Sighting

Notes

BLACK-THROATED GREEN WARBLER
Dendroica virens

Date of Sighting _____

Location of Sighting _____

_____

Notes

_____

_____

_____

_____

_____

_____

_____

_____

GOLDEN-CHEEKED WARBLER
Dendroica chrysoparia

Date of Sighting _____

Location of Sighting _____

_____

Notes

_____

_____

_____

_____

_____

_____

_____

BAY-BREASTED WARBLER
Dendroica castanea

Date of Sighting

Location of Sighting

Notes

BLACKPOLL WARBLER
Dendroica striata

Date of Sighting

Location of Sighting

Notes

KIRTLAND'S WARBLER
Dendroica kirtlandii

Date of Sighting

Location of Sighting

Notes

PRAIRIE WARBLER
Dendroica discolor

Date of Sighting

Location of Sighting

Notes

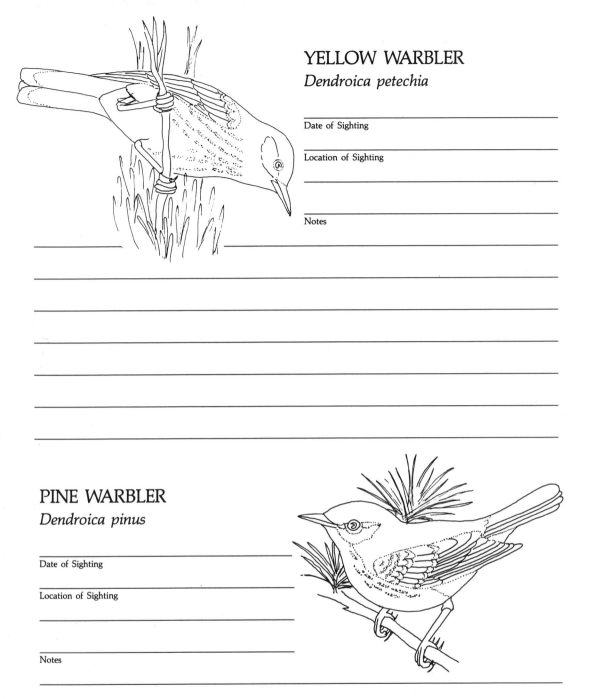

YELLOW WARBLER
Dendroica petechia

Date of Sighting

Location of Sighting

Notes

PINE WARBLER
Dendroica pinus

Date of Sighting

Location of Sighting

Notes

CERULEAN WARBLER
Dendroica cerulea

Date of Sighting

Location of Sighting

Notes

PALM WARBLER
Dendroica palmarum

Date of Sighting

Location of Sighting

Notes

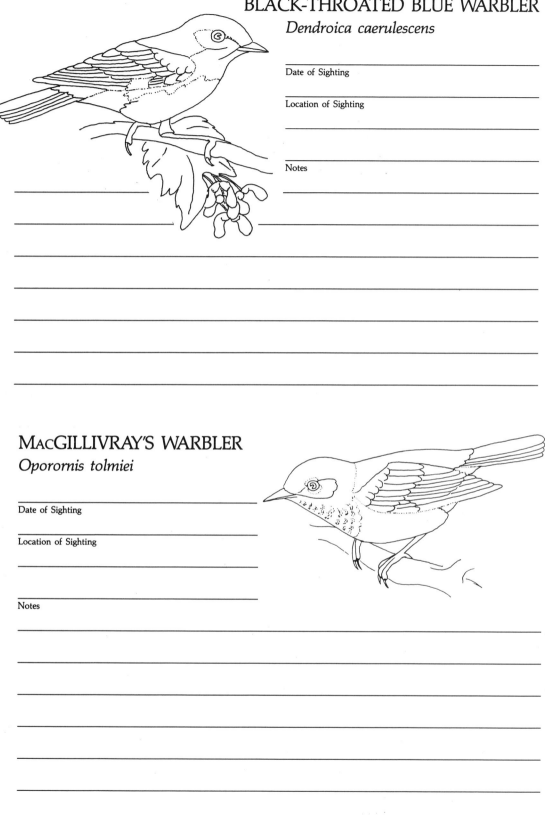

BLACK-THROATED BLUE WARBLER
Dendroica caerulescens

Date of Sighting

Location of Sighting

Notes

MACGILLIVRAY'S WARBLER
Oporornis tolmiei

Date of Sighting

Location of Sighting

Notes

MOURNING WARBLER
Oporornis philadelphia

Date of Sighting

Location of Sighting

Notes

KENTUCKY WARBLER
Oporornis formosus

Date of Sighting

Location of Sighting

Notes

CONNECTICUT WARBLER
Oporornis agilis

Date of Sighting

Location of Sighting

Notes

WILSON'S WARBLER
Wilsonia pusilla

Date of Sighting

Location of Sighting

Notes

CANADA WARBLER
Wilsonia canadensis

Date of Sighting

Location of Sighting

Notes

HOODED WARBLER
Wilsonia citrina

Date of Sighting

Location of Sighting

Notes

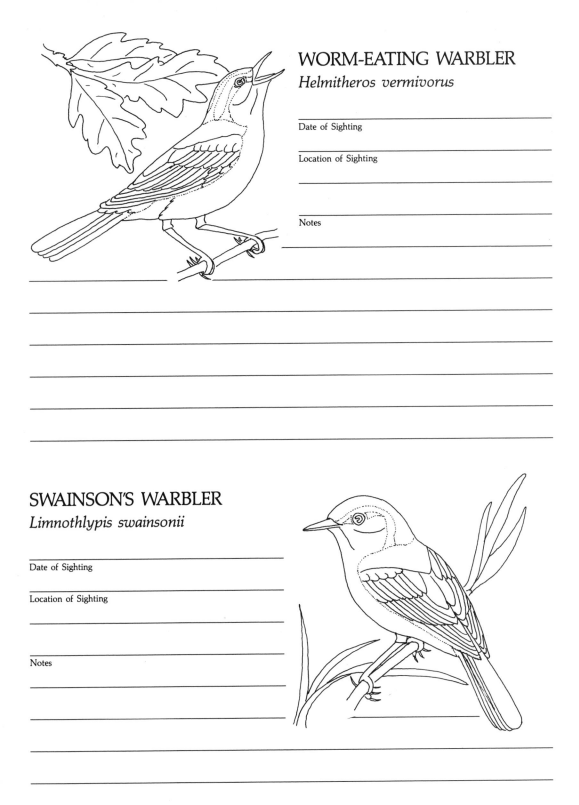

WORM-EATING WARBLER
Helmitheros vermivorus

Date of Sighting

Location of Sighting

Notes

SWAINSON'S WARBLER
Limnothlypis swainsonii

Date of Sighting

Location of Sighting

Notes

OVENBIRD
Seiurus aurocapillus

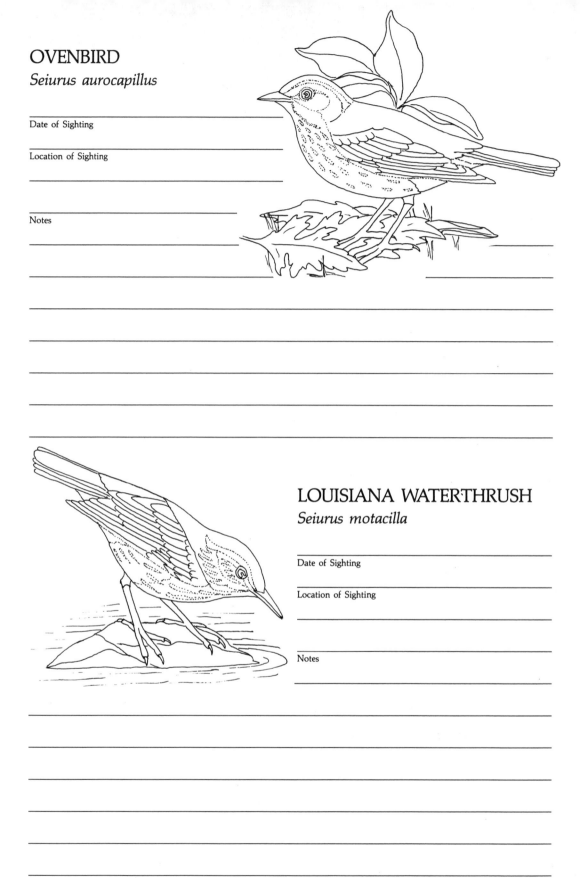

Date of Sighting

Location of Sighting

Notes

LOUISIANA WATERTHRUSH
Seiurus motacilla

Date of Sighting

Location of Sighting

Notes

NORTHERN WATERTHRUSH
Seiurus noveboracensis

Date of Sighting _____

Location of Sighting _____

_____

Notes _____

_____

_____

_____

_____

_____

_____

COMMON YELLOWTHROAT
Geothlypis trichas

Date of Sighting _____

Location of Sighting _____

_____

Notes _____

_____

_____

_____

_____

_____

_____

_____

_____

YELLOW-BREASTED CHAT
Icteria virens

Date of Sighting

Location of Sighting

Notes

AMERICAN REDSTART
Setophaga ruticilla

Date of Sighting

Location of Sighting

Notes

PAINTED REDSTART
Myioborus pictus

Date of Sighting

Location of Sighting

Notes

RED-FACED WARBLER
Cardellina rubrifrons

Date of Sighting

Location of Sighting

Notes

OLIVE WARBLER
Peucedramus taeniatus

Date of Sighting

Location of Sighting

Notes

ROSE-BREASTED GROSBEAK
Pheucticus ludovicianus

Date of Sighting

Location of Sighting

Notes

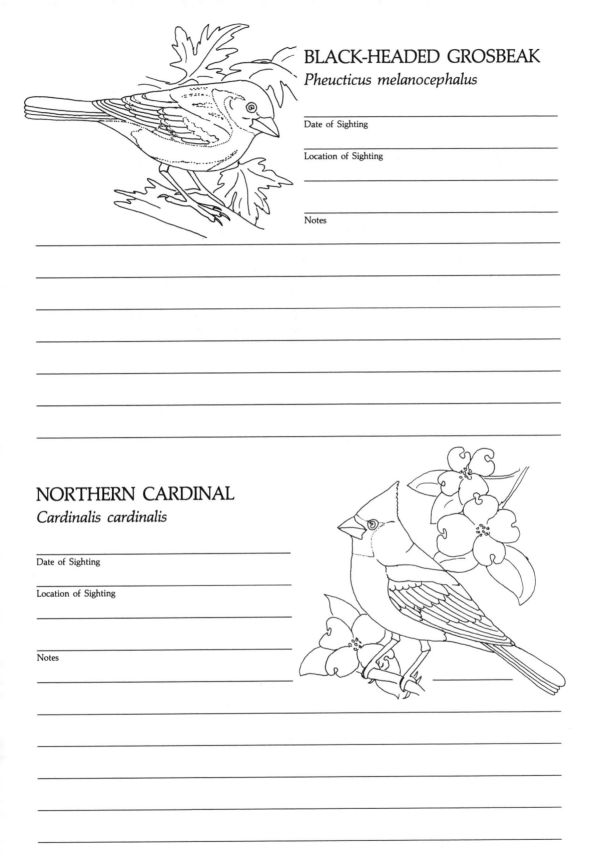

BLACK-HEADED GROSBEAK
Pheucticus melanocephalus

Date of Sighting

Location of Sighting

Notes

NORTHERN CARDINAL
Cardinalis cardinalis

Date of Sighting

Location of Sighting

Notes

PYRRHULOXIA
Cardinalis sinuatus

Date of Sighting

Location of Sighting

Notes

BLUE GROSBEAK
Guiraca caerulea

Date of Sighting

Location of Sighting

Notes

INDIGO BUNTING
Passerina cyanea

Date of Sighting

Location of Sighting

Notes

LAZULI BUNTING
Passerina amoena

Date of Sighting

Location of Sighting

Notes

PAINTED BUNTING
Passerina ciris

Date of Sighting

Location of Sighting

Notes

VARIED BUNTING
Passerina versicolor

Date of Sighting

Location of Sighting

Notes

BROWN TOWHEE
Pipilo fuscus

Date of Sighting

Location of Sighting

Notes

ABERT'S TOWHEE
Pipilo aberti

Date of Sighting

Location of Sighting

Notes

RUFOUS-SIDED TOWHEE
Pipilo erythrophthalmus

Date of Sighting

Location of Sighting

Notes

GREEN-TAILED TOWHEE
Pipilo chlorurus

Date of Sighting

Location of Sighting

Notes

SHARP-TAILED SPARROW
Ammodramus caudacutus

Date of Sighting

Location of Sighting

Notes

SEASIDE SPARROW
Ammodramus maritimus

Date of Sighting

Location of Sighting

Notes

HENSLOW'S SPARROW
Ammodramus henslowii

Date of Sighting

Location of Sighting

Notes

LE CONTE'S SPARROW
Ammodramus leconteii

Date of Sighting

Location of Sighting

Notes

GRASSHOPPER SPARROW
Ammodramus savannarum

Date of Sighting

Location of Sighting

Notes

BAIRD'S SPARROW
Ammodramus bairdii

Date of Sighting

Location of Sighting

Notes

VESPER SPARROW
Pooecetes gramineus

Date of Sighting

Location of Sighting

Notes

SAVANNAH SPARROW
Passerculus sandwichensis

Date of Sighting

Location of Sighting

Notes

SONG SPARROW
Melospiza melodia

Date of Sighting

Location of Sighting

Notes

LARK SPARROW
Chondestes grammacus

Date of Sighting

Location of Sighting

Notes

BLACK-THROATED SPARROW
Amphispiza bilineata

Date of Sighting

Location of Sighting

Notes

SAGE SPARROW
Amphispiza belli

Date of Sighting

Location of Sighting

Notes

RUFOUS-CROWNED SPARROW
Aimophila ruficeps

Date of Sighting

Location of Sighting

Notes

RUFOUS-WINGED SPARROW
Aimophila carpalis

Date of Sighting

Location of Sighting

Notes

CASSIN'S SPARROW
Aimophila cassinii

Date of Sighting

Location of Sighting

Notes

BACHMAN'S SPARROW
Aimophila aestivalis

Date of Sighting

Location of Sighting

Notes

AMERICAN TREE SPARROW
Spizella arborea

Date of Sighting

Location of Sighting

Notes

FIELD SPARROW
Spizella pusilla

Date of Sighting

Location of Sighting

Notes

CHIPPING SPARROW
Spizella passerina

Date of Sighting

Location of Sighting

Notes

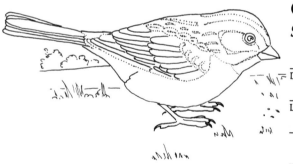

CLAY-COLORED SPARROW
Spizella pallida

Date of Sighting

Location of Sighting

Notes

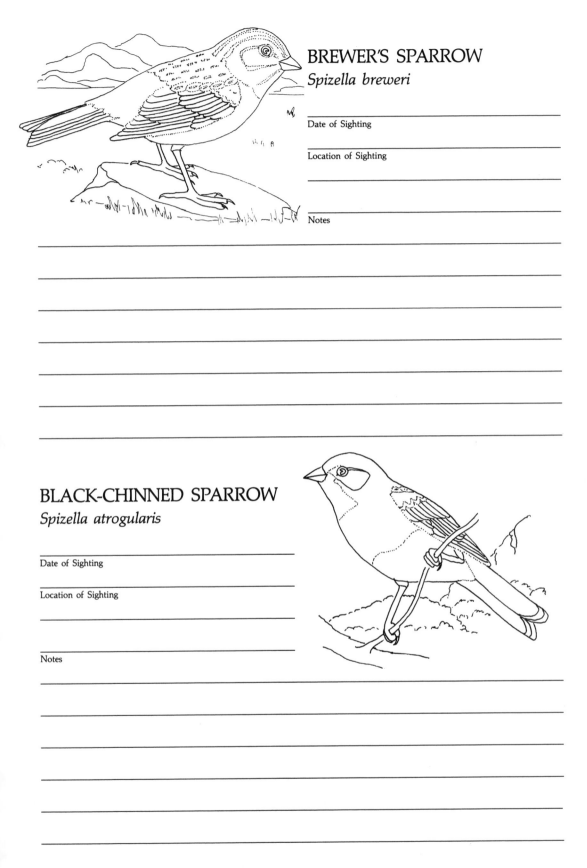

BREWER'S SPARROW
Spizella breweri

Date of Sighting

Location of Sighting

Notes

BLACK-CHINNED SPARROW
Spizella atrogularis

Date of Sighting

Location of Sighting

Notes

HARRIS' SPARROW
Zonotrichia querula

Date of Sighting

Location of Sighting

Notes

WHITE-THROATED SPARROW
Zonotrichia albicollis

Date of Sighting

Location of Sighting

Notes

WHITE-CROWNED SPARROW
Zonotrichia leucophrys

Date of Sighting

Location of Sighting

Notes

GOLDEN-CROWNED SPARROW
Zonotrichia atricapilla

Date of Sighting

Location of Sighting

Notes

FOX SPARROW
Passerella iliaca

Date of Sighting

Location of Sighting

Notes

LINCOLN'S SPARROW
Melospiza lincolnii

Date of Sighting

Location of Sighting

Notes

SWAMP SPARROW
Melospiza georgiana

Date of Sighting

Location of Sighting

Notes

YELLOW-EYED JUNCO
Junco phaeonotus

Date of Sighting

Location of Sighting

Notes

DARK-EYED JUNCO
Junco hyemalis

Date of Sighting

Location of Sighting

Notes

CHESTNUT-COLLARED LONGSPUR
Calcarius ornatus

Date of Sighting

Location of Sighting

Notes

LAPLAND LONGSPUR
Calcarius lapponicus

Date of Sighting

Location of Sighting

Notes

McCOWN'S LONGSPUR
Calcarius mccownii

Date of Sighting

Location of Sighting

Notes

SMITH'S LONGSPUR

Calcarius pictus

Date of Sighting _____

Location of Sighting _____

_____

_____

Notes

_____

_____

_____

_____

_____

_____

_____

_____

SNOW BUNTING

Plectrophenax nivalis

Date of Sighting _____

Location of Sighting _____

_____

_____

Notes _____

_____

_____

_____

_____

_____

_____

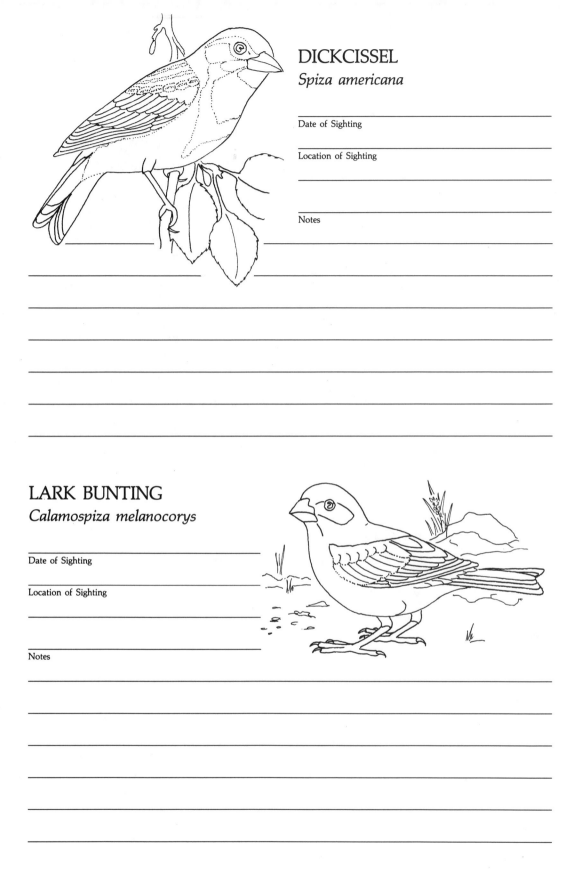

DICKCISSEL
Spiza americana

Date of Sighting

Location of Sighting

Notes

LARK BUNTING
Calamospiza melanocorys

Date of Sighting

Location of Sighting

Notes

WESTERN MEADOWLARK
Sturnella neglecta

Date of Sighting

Location of Sighting

Notes

YELLOW-HEADED BLACKBIRD
Xanthocephalus xanthocephalus

Date of Sighting

Location of Sighting

Notes

BOBOLINK
Dolichonyx oryzivorus

Date of Sighting

Location of Sighting

Notes

EASTERN MEADOWLARK
Sturnella magna

Date of Sighting

Location of Sighting

Notes

RUSTY BLACKBIRD
Euphagus carolinus

Date of Sighting _____

Location of Sighting _____

_____

Notes _____

_____

_____

_____

_____

_____

_____

_____

BREWER'S BLACKBIRD
Euphagus cyanocephalus

Date of Sighting _____

Location of Sighting _____

_____

Notes _____

_____

_____

_____

_____

_____

_____

_____

_____

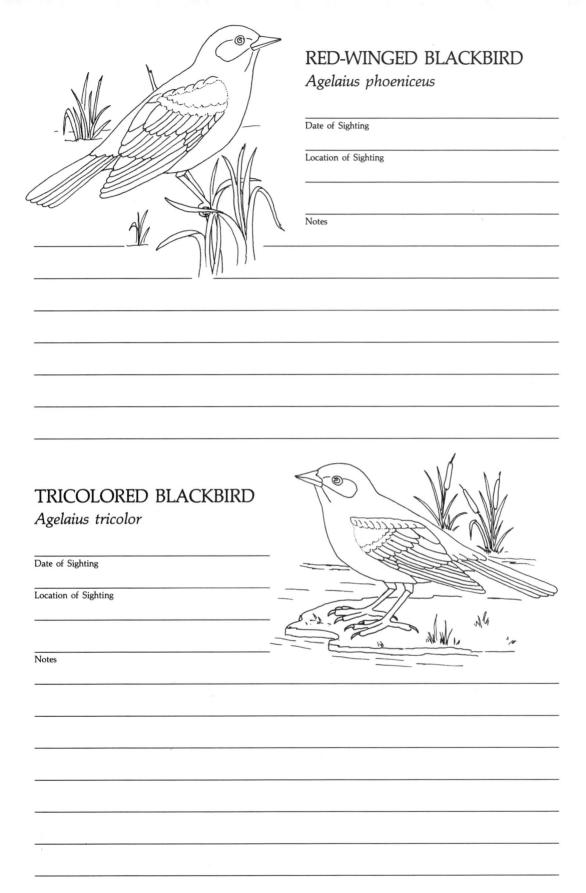

RED-WINGED BLACKBIRD
Agelaius phoeniceus

Date of Sighting

Location of Sighting

Notes

TRICOLORED BLACKBIRD
Agelaius tricolor

Date of Sighting

Location of Sighting

Notes

BRONZED COWBIRD
Molothrus aeneus

Date of Sighting

Location of Sighting

Notes

BROWN-HEADED COWBIRD
Molothrus ater

Date of Sighting

Location of Sighting

Notes

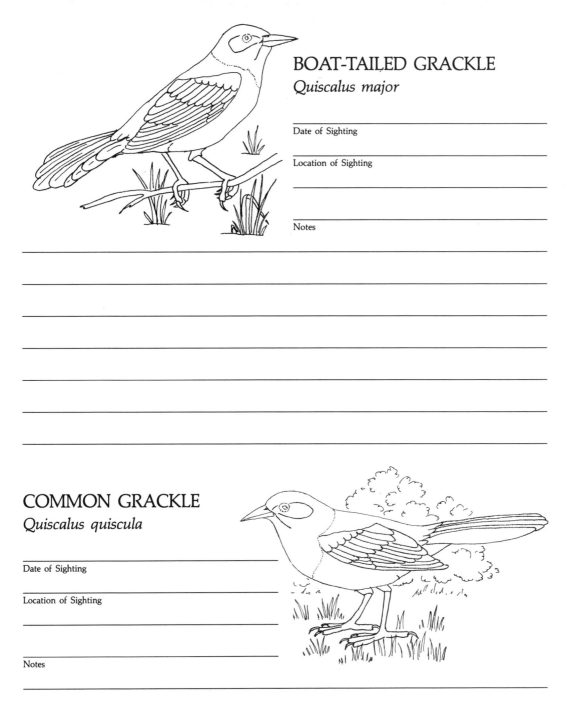

BOAT-TAILED GRACKLE
Quiscalus major

Date of Sighting

Location of Sighting

Notes

COMMON GRACKLE
Quiscalus quiscula

Date of Sighting

Location of Sighting

Notes

GREAT-TAILED GRACKLE
Quiscalus mexicanus

Date of Sighting

Location of Sighting

Notes

SCOTT'S ORIOLE
Icterus parisorum

Date of Sighting

Location of Sighting

Notes

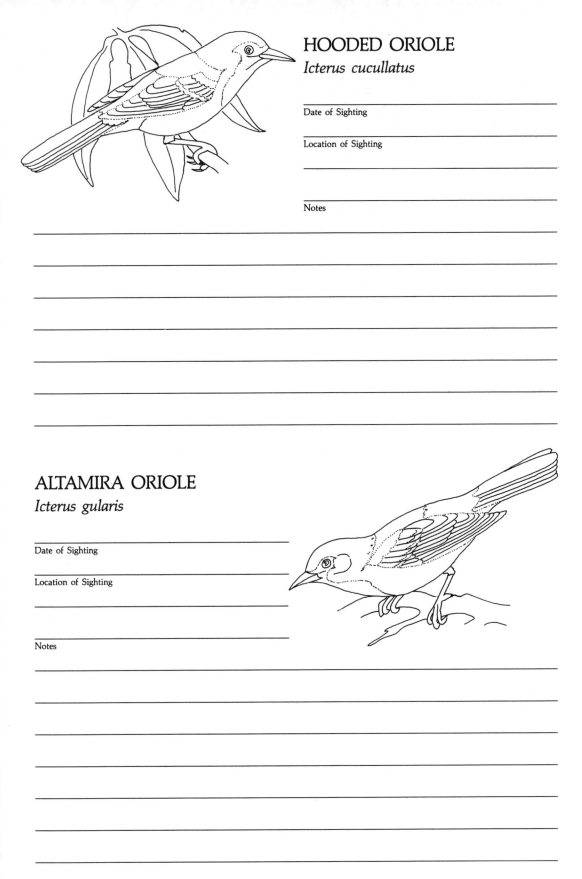

HOODED ORIOLE
Icterus cucullatus

Date of Sighting

Location of Sighting

Notes

ALTAMIRA ORIOLE
Icterus gularis

Date of Sighting

Location of Sighting

Notes

ORCHARD ORIOLE
Icterus spurius

Date of Sighting

Location of Sighting

Notes

NORTHERN ORIOLE
Icterus galbula

Date of Sighting

Location of Sighting

Notes

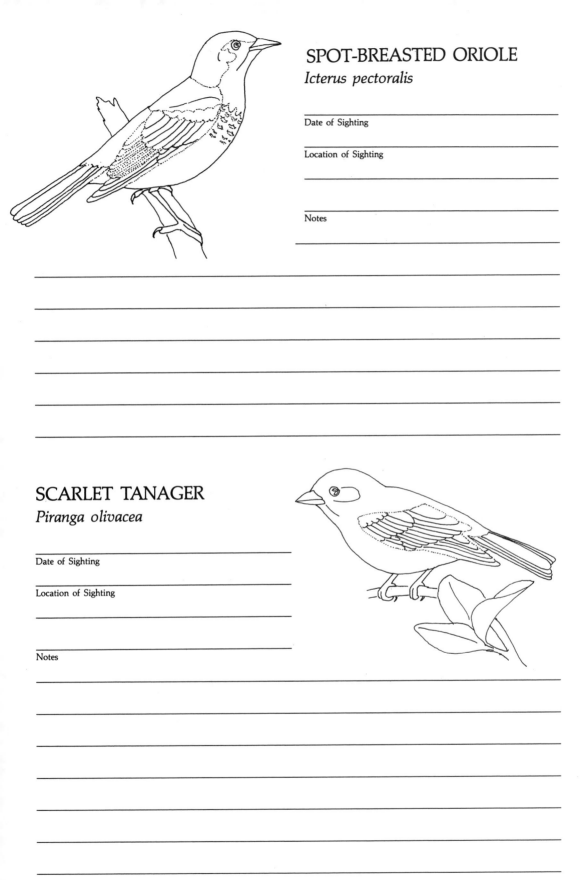

SPOT-BREASTED ORIOLE
Icterus pectoralis

Date of Sighting

Location of Sighting

Notes

SCARLET TANAGER
Piranga olivacea

Date of Sighting

Location of Sighting

Notes

HEPATIC TANAGER
Piranga flava

Date of Sighting

Location of Sighting

Notes

WESTERN TANAGER
Piranga ludoviciana

Date of Sighting

Location of Sighting

Notes

SUMMER TANAGER
Piranga ruba

Date of Sighting

Location of Sighting

Notes

WEAVERS
(PASSERIDAE)

Weavers

The English or house sparrow is no more characteristic of England than the Guinea fowl is characteristic of Guinea. Both exotics got their popular names from the country that supplied the first birds to places where they were introduced. In 1850, and again in 1852, Nicolas Pike released house sparrows imported from England around his home in Brooklyn, New York, with the hope they'd destroy the cankerworms which periodically ravaged his shade trees. The avian immigrants did more than eat cankerworms; by 1900, house sparrows were established from coast to coast.

This species is a true weaver, not a sparrow, and builds a weaver-like covered nest, unless it finds a prefabricated cavity. When I was a boy growing up in Forest Hills, English sparrows established sizeable nesting colonies in the ivy growing on the sides of my family's house, and their loud cheepings and chirpings were the most familiar bird sounds of my youth. House sparrows have declined somewhat since reaching population peaks at mid-century, and you're as likely now to see house finches as house sparrows at suburban bird feeders.

EURASIAN TREE SPARROW
Passer Montanus

Date of Sighting

Location of Sighting

Notes

HOUSE SPARROW
Passer domesticus

Date of Sighting

Location of Sighting

Notes

FINCHES
(FRINGILLIDAE)

Finches

The industry of packaged bird-seed and assembly-line feeders is a post-World War II phenomenon. Yet all but one of the North American birds in this Family have scientific names referring to their feeding habits, suggesting that the pioneering naturalists who named the birds may also have provided them with winter fare. And certainly no birds are more reliable habitues of feeders than the finches.

Six of the family are *Carduelis* from the Latin *carduus*, meaning "thistle," the goldfinch's favorite food. Three of the family are *Carpodacus*, meaning "fruit biter," which would seem to be a silly name for a seed eater, except that etymologist, Ernest A. Choate, points out that these finches are, indeed, not adverse to biting fruit. *Loxia* refers to the "crooked" mandibles of the crossbill, an adaptation for extracting pine seeds. *Pinicola enucleator* is the "pine inhabitor who husks pine seeds." And *Coccothraustes vespertinus* is the "western" or "evening" (referring to the western sky where the evening sun sets) "kernel crusher."

The rosy finch is the only Family member which escapes the food connection. Its scientific name even escapes commonsense. *Leucosticte* means "varied white" in Greek and refers to the bird's allegedly white plumage. The rosy finch, however, is black, brown, pink and even gray on the face and back of the head. But white? That's Greek to me!

PINE SISKIN
Carduelis pinus

Date of Sighting

Location of Sighting

Notes

AMERICAN GOLDFINCH
Carduelis tristis

Date of Sighting

Location of Sighting

Notes

LESSER GOLDFINCH
Carduelis psaltria

Date of Sighting

Location of Sighting

Notes

LAWRENCE'S GOLDFINCH
Carduelis lawrencei

Date of Sighting

Location of Sighting

Notes

HOARY REDPOLL
Carduelis hornemanni

Date of Sighting

Location of Sighting

Notes

COMMON REDPOLL
Carduelis flammea

Date of Sighting

Location of Sighting

Notes

WHITE-WINGED CROSSBILL
Loxia leucoptera

Date of Sighting

Location of Sighting

Notes

RED CROSSBILL
Loxia curvirostra

Date of Sighting

Location of Sighting

Notes

PINE GROSBEAK
Pinicola enucleator

Date of Sighting

Location of Sighting

Notes

ROSY FINCH
Leucosticte arctoa

Date of Sighting

Location of Sighting

Notes

PURPLE FINCH
Carpodacus purpureus

Date of Sighting

Location of Sighting

Notes

CASSIN'S FINCH
Carpodacus cassinii

Date of Sighting

Location of Sighting

Notes

HOUSE FINCH
Carpodacus mexicanus

Date of Sighting

Location of Sighting

Notes

EVENING GROSBEAK
Coccothraustes vespertinus

Date of Sighting

Location of Sighting

Notes

INDEX AND CHECKLIST

Alphabetical by Common Name